W9-AAR-602

DRINKING DISTILLED

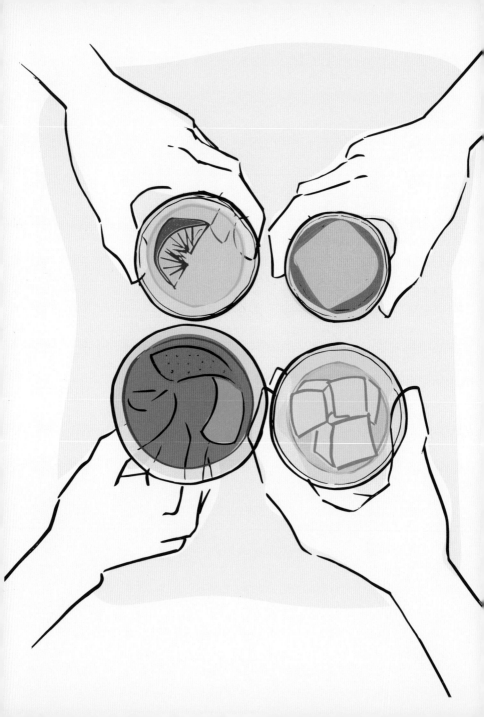

DISCARD

DRINKING DISTILLED

A USER'S MANUAL

JEFFREY MORGENTHALER

ILLUSTRATIONS BY SAMI GASTON

TEN SPEED PRESS
California | New York

To every bartender I've ever had the pleasure of working with over the past twenty-two years:

Annette "Netty" Lee Lee, Mrs. Bertini, Lila, Becky, Sarah, and Holly at The Tiny Tavern.

Jimmy, Timmy, Old Richard, Erin, Cindy, Nate, and Mairz at The Vet's Club.

Big Mike for four whole days at The Black Forest.

Carmella, Kai, and Ray at Neighbors.

Adrian, Kim, Dave "Ira Glass" Faigin, and Coffee Matt at Bamboo.

Lynette for four shifts at Chanterelle.

Watson and other Adrian at Marché.

Chancho, Sarge, Zeb, and Hebb at Red Agave.

Kelly, Starla, Adam, and, of course, Scooter at El Vaquero.

Rico and Scooter (again) at Bel Ami.

Cappy, Ansel, Pike, Syd, Jonny, Sanger, Banjo, Angie, Frankie, Junebug, Becks, Turtle Burger, Sharky, Shooter, and Nate at Clyde Common.

"Baby's Treat" Gordon, Amy Jo, Handsome Josh, Brandy, Jamie, Suze, Meals, and Travvy and DPG at Pepe Le Moko.

And most of all, Breakfast Sami, who got so sick of working brunch that she gave up on tending bar entirely, started drawing again, and let me talk her into doing the illustrations for this book.

CONTENTS

Introduction

Right around the time of my twenty-first birthday, I began taking a mild interest in bars and drinking. I'd never really explored alcohol or bars. I wasn't one of those cool kids in high school who got invited to drink cheap beer out of a can, standing around in a field, thumbs in jean pockets, spitting tobacco on the ground. That's how kids drank in rural areas like mine back in the '80s.

When I got to community college, I never really thought about getting a fake ID and hitting the bars. That just seemed like something older kids did, and I was too busy drinking Mountain Dew, riding a skateboard (still), and playing Led Zeppelin songs on my acoustic guitar.

That's not to say bars didn't seem interesting to me. Bars were for cool people, or so I thought, and were sort of exclusive in the sense that kids in the next-older age bracket went there. It was like a private club, and I was on the outside, looking in with my Christian Hosoi Hammerhead skate deck in hand.

I began studying interior architecture at the University of Oregon, in Eugene, right around the time I turned twenty-one; I was then very interested in bars and allowed inside the inner sanctum. I remember my tame twenty-first birthday: I rounded up the two or three people I knew who were old enough to drink, and we went to my first bar—Rennie's Landing, the closest bar to campus. We split a pitcher of beer, awkwardly watched the crowd (which seemed right at home in a bar), and promptly went home.

I went to a few bars over the next couple of years, but I was too poor to get the full experience and probably too awkward to care. The defining moment of my drinking education came in 1996, when, in an effort to save up some money and maybe meet some girls, I got my first job in a bar: The Tiny Tavern, in Eugene. I was the most nervous, awkward, twenty-four-year-old bartender you have ever seen, pouring only beer and making chili, because that's just about all we sold.

Over the next four years, while I finished my degree in interior architecture and worked part-time in architecture firms and at the tavern, I learned more about the inner workings of hard-drinking journeymen than most people three times my age.

After having my life threatened on multiple occasions, and thanks to the rise of swing dancing and atomic cocktails, I was ready to move on to working in a proper cocktail lounge. And so, I got a job at the local VFW hall slinging highballs for veterans and hipsters. We had a jukebox full of everything from the Clash to Big Bad Voodoo Daddy, and I learned a lot about making really simple cocktails very quickly.

I also picked up a lot of bad habits and learned some blatantly incorrect information. On my first day, I was sent to pick up some citrus at the supermarket across the street. When I came back, the bar matriarch informed me that limes are nothing more than lemons that haven't fully ripened yet (wrong). And it was probably a year or two after I moved on and started to work in proper restaurant bars that I realized you don't pack the ice down in the glass with the palm of your hand, a trick club bartenders use to make a drink seem stronger. I just thought that was protocol.

At one point, I thought I was the world's most informed bartender when it came to the art of the martini, until I humiliated myself in front of a bartender who was chilling my glass with ice as I sat in front of her well. "Oh, no ice, please. Up," I blurted. I still want to die every time I think about that. She was so good at making drinks, such a badass bartender. I was so dumb, so cocky.

If only I'd had someone to teach me all that I would later glean over the course of twenty-two years behind and in front of the bar. I could also have saved myself the embarrassment of the time I thought Mountain Dew was a good mixer for gin. Or the years I spent telling everyone that tequila was made from a cactus.

I can't go back and change my past misinformation, but I can shape *your* future understanding. And so here it is, just about everything you need to know in order to get started drinking well.

01.

GENERAL INSTRUC- TIONS

I didn't learn too much about how to drink from my parents, save for some seasonal considerations (piña coladas in the summer, Bailey's and coffee in the winter). There's such a taboo regarding drinking in the United States that, most of the time, alcohol is hidden from children. European youth, on the other hand, are taught to appreciate wine at an early age, and though their overall alcohol consumption may be greater than ours, their incidents of binge drinking are far less. One possible reason is that alcohol is inextricably tied to dining culture on that continent, whereas it's connected to party culture on ours. Rates of alcohol-related deaths are far lower in countries such as Spain, Portugal, and Italy than in the U.S., where drinking well is something of a lost art. And, while customs and mores are always bound by change, there are some traditions that still bear following. I firmly believe that if we could take a little more time to celebrate the ritual of sharing a drink in this country, and spend less energy focusing on being drunk, we all might be able to enjoy life a little more. And that's a side effect worth having.

GUIDELINES TO HEED

If you ever begin to look around for advice on drinking, you're guaranteed to discover a whole world of garbage guidelines from current or former bartenders who are so beyond the point of burnout that they have no right to be proffering advice to anyone. *Stand at attention. Have your money ready. Tip a certain number of dollars per drink.*

I've always found such advice to be in poor taste. What really helps people? Drinking advice you can actually use. So here's my attempt to mitigate all the ill-advised, self-serving bullshit advice you're going to get elsewhere.

Toasting

If you ordered and paid for the round, it's your right and responsibility to make a toast. And before I go on, let me just remind you that "toasting" or "making a toast" is how you say that. "Cheers" is not a verb, it's a type of toast. So you might be saying "cheers" when you toast, but you're not "cheersing." Please stop demanding that people "cheers" you. Ask your friend if they'll raise a glass with you or allow you to make a toast.

Whew. Now that I've gotten that little pet peeve off my chest, let's continue.

Everyone has their tradition. Some people insist on tapping the glass to the table after clinking glasses. Others say that you need to make eye contact with everyone toasting in order to preserve your luck and integrity. While I believe in making eye contact with my friends, I can't stand it when someone thinks they need to go around the circle enforcing it. Nobody needs a compliance officer watching their every move while they're drinking.

It's always good to have a simple toast in your back pocket for occasions when you're in charge of speaking before the drink. And really, it doesn't matter what it is. It could be as simple as "Here's to you!" or as complex as an Irish soliloquy, but I find that these are little more than stand-ins when you have little to nothing good to say. If you can, speak from the heart, say something nice about how much you enjoy the company, and, for the love of alcohol, keep it short. Nobody wants to listen to you drone on with their glass in the air, mere inches from their mouth.

Gendered Drinking

Night after night, bartenders and drinkers everywhere are forced to listen to men sharing their bullshit opinions of everyone else's drink order. Someone in their party ordered their whiskey on the rocks? Time to let them know they're drinking whiskey the wrong way. A man having a glass of rosé wine? Time to freak out because it's pink.

This idea that certain drinks are for men and others are for women is so tired. A chilled glass of rosé, with its slightly more tannic character (which comes from grape skin contact during the fermentation process) is a killer drink on a warm spring or summer day. I put ice in my whiskey about half the time. It doesn't make me any less tough or show I know any less about whiskey. I know more about whiskey than most guys, but I don't consider that a gender identity statement.

What's really sad to me is the idea that using a stemmed glass is somehow demeaning to the drinker. "But I'll just spill it" is a justification that I hear nightly. Listen, using a stemmed wine glass or cocktail glass is the sign of a real grown-up, male or female. If you can't use a stemmed wine or cocktail glass without feeling emasculated or spilling your drink everywhere, you should go home and practice. This is a skill you should have learned in college.

Glassware

There's no shortage of glassware out there to sip spirits from, and there's certainly no shortage of articles written about which glasses are "correct" for sipping things like whiskey or cognac. And just about every year there seems to be a new crop of both.

Brandy snifters are good for storing vintage matchbooks, or making a tiny terrarium. They're this old-timey, really dumb option for tasting spirits, a holdover from God-knows-when, and their main selling point is that they are designed to warm up the liquid, thereby vaporizing the alcohol. Hey, you know what you don't want to smell when you're trying to enjoy a spirit served neat? Pure alcohol. Pure alcohol smells like the inside of your nose burning and not much else.

The ideal glass for evaluating spirits on the nose and palate (our overly fancy language for smelling and tasting) allows you to smell and taste[1] the actual flavors in the spirit and not just pure alcohol. In the words of cartoon propane salesman Hank Hill, you want to "taste the meat, not the heat."

So ditch the snifter and use one of the many other, better options out there. Seriously, a coffee mug is a better choice for tasting spirits than a snifter. There are a few options that I really like (see the illustration, opposite). You can easily find them online.

Drinking Games

When I say "drinking games," I'm not referring to playing chess, checkers, Monopoly, cornhole, or even Cards Against Humanity with your friends while you're having drinks. You know exactly what I'm talking about. Drinking games that are designed for one

---

1 When my colleagues and I evaluate spirits for work, we do everything we can to taste past the burn of the pure alcohol. Beyond choosing the right glassware, this also means not aerating the spirit by pulling air in through your mouth the way you might do with wine. Spirits are best experienced by letting the liquid gently rest on the tongue and throughout the mouth and then spitting it out.

purpose: to get everyone playing extremely drunk whether they want to be or not.

If you're in college and you're playing drinking games, you're fine. We've all been there. But once you graduate, or reach an age commensurate with someone who has a bachelor's degree, you've got to knock it off with the drinking games. You're a grown-up now, and grown-ups (a) drink at their own pace, (b) engage in conversation with other grown-ups while drinking, and (c) participate in games of leisure, such as golf or horseshoes, while they drink.

So the rule I'm proposing is this: make the weekend after your first week at your first real job the last time you play Quarters, Beer Pong, Flip Cup, Asshole, Roxanne (or Jammin'), Three Man, and especially Wizard Staff or Edward Fortyhands. Or, ideally, wean yourself while you're still in college and before you go out into the world.

Privacy

I was fortunate to have gone through most of my heavy drinking years at a time before everyone carried cameras around in their pockets and long before cameras became connected to the internet at all times. That's not to say that there aren't a few choice photos out there of me at my prime idiocy, but fortunately most of them are not digital.

Decide whether you're going to allow photographs while drinking and whether you care about strangers being able to see you, if at not your absolute worst, then rarely at your best.

Barfing

This should probably read "No Shots," but you and I both know that isn't going to prevent you from doing them. Seriously, you've had alcohol before. You know when you're going to barf. So know your limit and leave before you do it, if you're going to. Because I can tell you, nothing—and I mean nothing—kills the vibe of every single person in the room like the smell of vomit. So you could potentially be remembered as the person who ruined everyone's Saturday night. Think about that.

And this isn't to say that you shouldn't feel free to get drunk from time to time; but do keep in mind that when you vomit, whether it's at home or out in public, someone will be required to clean it up. Drink accordingly and remember that you can always clean up your own mess in the morning if you're at home. Hey, at least it'll be a lesson you won't soon forget.

Using the Irish Good-bye

There is something so elegant, so subtle, so brilliant about the Irish Good-bye. If you're not familiar with this particular term, allow me to explain. The Irish Good-bye (or French Exit, in some circles) is an offensive term for an inoffensive operation. It's the act of leaving a bar or party without letting your friends know that you're leaving.

The reason for this is simple: your friends are monsters and will do everything in their power to keep you at the bar after you have decided, with a still somewhat clear head, that it is time for you to go home.

The methodology is simple: excuse yourself for a moment, whether it be to use the restroom, to step outside for a cigarette or phone call, or to go on some vague errand (these are drunk people you're dealing with; you don't need to be super clear here). Then, once you've broken away from the group, make your exit. Hop on the bus, Gus. Hail a taxi or use your ridesharing app. Catch a ride from a sober friend. Just get home as quickly as possible.

You will be given endless amounts of grief for this. There will be phone calls and text messages once they've discovered you've gone. There might even be idle threats, and there will certainly be claims that you're missing a good time, but you must stay strong. If you need to turn off your phone, by all means do so. Because then something funny will happen the next morning: everyone will envy you for making the right choice, and they might even let you know so.

Act humble; don't be too smug.

Drinking and Driving

Every year, around ten thousand people in the United States are killed as a result of someone driving drunk.[2] And many of those people were not the ones who had been drinking irresponsibly. Most people admit to having driven under the influence at least once in their lives, and hopefully that was the last time they did it.

Not only is driving under the influence of alcohol careless, irresponsible, and absolutely unforgivable, but in this day and age, it is also unnecessary. We have more options for getting around safely right now than ever in history. For the price of a couple of drinks, a safe and reliable ride can be magically summoned, in minutes, from your phone.

2 National Highway Traffic Safety Administration, 2014

Drunk driving costs the United States $199 billion per year.[3] If you consider yourself to be one of those people who cares about the country or the economy, and you drive after drinking, you are part of a massive problem that can be easily solved.

I am so passionate about this topic that I have ended romantic relationships and friendships with people who insist on drinking and driving. It is a sign of the most selfish, thoughtless sort of individual, and you deserve to surround yourself with better people than that. Get your friends and loved ones home safely, encourage others to do the same, and let's all make this very real problem go away once and for all.

Hangovers

Hangovers come in more types, styles, and varieties than does rain in the Pacific Northwest. I've often enjoyed a good, sporty hangover, but I think we've all had hangovers that have been so brutally aggressive that we've named them and remembered them like they were our high school bullies.

The terrible news is that we still don't know exactly what causes a hangover. I mean, if we did, we could cure it, and that would mark the beginning of the largest party in the history of human civilization. That's probably never going to happen. But we do know a few tricks to help ease the pain.

---

3 National Highway Traffic Safety Administration, 2014

The simplest answer is that alcohol is a diuretic. This one's fun to explain. When you consume alcohol, your pituitary gland ceases production of a hormone called vasopressin. Vasopressin tells you not to pee. In the absence of vasopressin, your body expels upward of four times the liquid it receives. So for every glass of wine you consume, you're peeing out potentially a whole wine bottle of water! This is why everyone tells you to drink water—because alcohol is inherently dehydrating.

When you become dehydrated, your brain loses enough water to literally shrink. Try not to think about this the next time you're suffering the ravages of an alcohol-induced head pounder. Your brain's membrane, the one that attaches it to the inside of your skull, is inflamed by your dehydrated, shrunken raisin of a brain as it pulls away from your cranium.

But that's right about where our understanding of hangovers stops. Some science points to the toxin acetaldehyde, a by-product of the way our bodies break down alcohol, but other studies can't seem to nail down a correlation between acetaldehyde levels and hangover severity. And it's not necessarily true that triple-, quintuple-, or gazillion-times–distilled vodka goes any easier on you than the *congeners*[4] found in red wine, a notorious villain in the drinking world.

----

4 A congener is any by-product of the fermentation or distillation process other than ethyl alcohol. Some people like to refer to them as "impurities," but I prefer to think of them as the compounds that give drinks their wonderful flavors.

I can assure you that "Liquor before beer, never fear; beer before liquor, never sicker" is a myth as well. Your body doesn't care what order you consume different flavors of ethyl alcohol. I imagine that adage comes from the fact that spirits contain more alcohol than beer, and consuming liquor at the end of the night rather than the beginning probably signifies that you're doing shots. And yeah, binge drinking is certainly going to give you a hangover.

And that's what it comes down to in the end: I'm really sorry to break the bad news to you, but the only 100 percent reliable, scientifically proven method for guaranteeing that you never have a hangover is not to drink. But let's admit it, you and I both know that's probably not going to happen.

Teetotaling

You've made plans, aligned schedules, and finally you're getting together with a group of friends for a night of partying. Things are going as planned, everyone is at the bar, drinks are starting to flow, and then suddenly someone in your group orders a soda water or—gasp—a virgin cocktail. How dare they not join you in consuming alcohol, right?

Look, nothing screams, "I'm a giant child" like complaining that someone else isn't drinking. I've shown up to parties with a six-pack of nonalcoholic beer and gotten some very real glares from people who thought that my desire to not drink had the slightest thing to do with them.

Let me tell you: not everyone drinks all of the time. Often, the thought of day-drinking is repulsive to me. My favorite pizza pairing is actually root beer, not real beer. And sometimes people are pregnant and not ready to talk about it yet. There are a million reasons someone might choose not to have a drink, and none of them should be any concern of yours.

We, as enlightened drinkers, do not harass others for not partaking alongside us. It's not going to ruin your night, so let it go.

02.

WHAT
YOU'RE
DRINKING

Alcohol has always been shrouded in mystery, myth, and legend, and I'd say this is more true about booze than anything else we consume. Think about the conversations regarding food: gluten is the devil, eggs are deemed alternately healthy or unhealthy every other year, sugar gives you cancer, "free radicals" are conspiring to poison your cells, and antioxidants are found in superfoods (whatever that means).

None of that even compares with the conversations you overhear every night at the bar: Gin is made from juniper (it's not; it's just flavored with juniper, a subtle difference). "Brown" liquor is brown because it's full of impurities (it's not). Absinthe makes you hallucinate (it doesn't). Even that fish-lipped bar "expert" from the reality show says tequila is a hallucinogen (it's not).

And yet at the same time, many self-proclaimed liquor geeks will inform you that you need to know all sorts of arcane BS about spirits and cocktails, which is a great deal more than I've selected to share with you here. But you don't. Because at some point, it's the law of diminishing returns; you don't need a chemical engineering degree specializing in distillation to select a whiskey that you enjoy. And it's unimportant to know exactly when and how the martini was invented to make the best one in the world. Even I can't remember half that stuff, so I just remember what's important and leave out the rest.

At some basic level, we all want to know what we're putting in our bodies. I'd like to think that just about any reasonable person would have a train of thought along the lines of *Since I'm about to have something that alters my state of mind, I guess I should know a thing or two about it.* But not everyone is as thoughtful as you and I are.

And so to that end, what follows is the basics: facts about alcohol to know, some myths to debunk in an effort to demystify spirits and cocktails, and enough information to keep you informed as you navigate the vast territory of all things booze related.

DRINKING SPIRITS

To truly understand alcohol, it's important to know where it comes from because one of the biggest myths that pervades drinking culture is the idea that different types of drinks come from radically different things. And really, that's just not true.

All of the alcohol in the world that humans drink is made from fermentation, which is the process of yeast eating sugar and converting it into ethyl alcohol. That's it. And I do mean all of it. Belgian beer to dark rum to Champagne, Scotch whisky, red wine, or Smirnoff Ice—it's all made from ethyl alcohol, which is created when yeast eats sugar.

When yeast is introduced to any type of sugar, whether it's the sugar found in wheat, red wine grapes, the agave plant, or even yak's milk, alcohol and carbon dioxide are created. They're, uh, the yeast cell's waste products. Carbon dioxide and alcohol are, quite literally, the burps and poop that are excreted when yeast consumes sugar. Drink up!

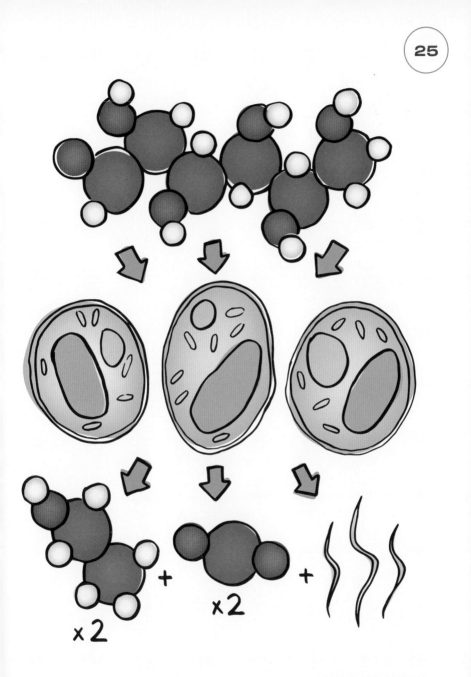

WHAT YOU'RE DRINKING

DRINKING DISTILLED

Sugar

The sugars that yeast eats and from which alcohol is derived generally come from plants. There is a small group of spirits made from animal products, but that's about it. Whiskey and rum are always made from grasses. Wine, brandy, and tequila are always made from fruits. Vodka can be made from most anything; there is even a bunch of them made from milk. Yes, milk.

What fermentation does is to create a sort of beer (for things fermented from grasses) or wine (for things fermented from fruit). In fact, in the distillation world, those two terms are used to describe pretty much anything fermented, even if it's not the end product. Whiskey makers refer to the stuff they ultimately make whiskey from as "beer"; cognac producers talk about "wine." It's all the same stuff.

Thinking about alcohol in this way, in terms of the raw materials that it's made from, helps me understand it better while keeping it very simple. Different materials create very different flavors, so having some sense of where your drink comes from helps you understand even more deeply how it tastes as a spirit, and why.

Distillation

Fermentation has an upper limit of around 15% alcohol by volume (ABV), which is about the maximum amount of alcohol

that yeast can survive in before it dies. To get up to a higher ABV, say, in order to make whiskey or vodka or rum, the alcohol that is created by fermentation (and remember, all of the alcohol that we drink comes from fermentation) must be distilled. But what does that even mean?

Distillation is the process of separating alcohol (with a boiling point of 173.1°F) from water (with a boiling point of 212°F) and any remaining solids. You're taking advantage of the fact that alcohol and water have different boiling points and using that to separate them. So you just heat your beer or wine or whatever above 173.1°F but below 212.1°F, and the alcohol will boil off for you to capture, but the water and other stuff won't. That's really all distillation is, at its core.

Aging

Every single spirit looks exactly the same after distillation;
they're all clear and colorless, like water. That's because the
final product after distillation is little more than ethyl alcohol,
water, and some flavors. In most cases, color comes in when
spirits are stored in wooden barrels.

It's probably a happy coincidence that storing a spirit in an oak barrel for some period of time mellows it, softens its rough edges, and tames some of its flaws. Prior to the use of oak barrels to transport spirits, booze was typically stored in stoneware or glass, which doesn't contribute much in terms of aging, thanks to their airtight, nonporous nature.

Most barrels are toasted or charred to some degree before use, and this toasting helps add color to the final product. The toasting creates a layer of caramelized wood sugars inside the cask, so what distilleries are doing over the course of many years is using the spirit as a solvent to wash caramelized sugar out of the barrel. That caramelized sugar is pretty much all that the brown color is in so-called "brown" liquor.

It's funny to me that so much fuss is made about brown liquor, the color of which is almost always all natural, while little attention is paid to the artificial coloring and chemicals people consume on a daily basis. Farmed salmon is usually dyed, since natural pink color comes from a wild diet. Pickles are almost always colored for consistency. Inexpensive cheese typically contains coloring, and unless you're making your breakfast from whole foods you picked up at the farmers' market, you're definitely consuming a whole mess of chemicals. Protein shakes? Flavored yogurt? And still, people freak out about caramelized wood sugars from the oak barrel their bourbon was aged in. Come on.

Naming

Many alcoholic beverages have strict regional (among other) requirements in order to be called what they're called. For instance, everyone knows that sparkling wine needs to be from the Champagne region of France in order to be called Champagne (and not sparkling wine or *méthode champenoise*). But there are many more rules, and a few myths (of course), in spirit naming.

BRANDY is a spirit made from fruit, any fruit. COGNAC is a special type of brandy made only from grapes in the Cognac region of France. MEZCAL is also a type of brandy made from the heart of many types of agave plant. TEQUILA is a special type of mezcal made only from Weber Blue Agave, in the Jalisco region of Mexico.[1] RUM is a spirit made from sugarcane or sugarcane by-products. RHUM AGRICOLE is made from fresh-pressed sugarcane juice, made only on the island of Martinique.

Whisk(e)y

One of the most complicated categories of spirit is whiskey, as it's probably the largest category in the world and encompasses many, many different types of spirit, most of which taste wildly different from each other. At its most basic level, whiskey is

1   Yes, there are many other rules about this one.

a spirit made from grain and then aged in barrels. Within that framework, most of the biggest differences in whiskies are regional. They are generally classified by country of origin first: American whiskey, Scotch whisky, Irish whiskey, Canadian whisky, and so on. Within each country, whiskies are then sometimes classified by style.

There's SCOTCH WHISKY (the Scottish spell it without an "e"—it's not a big deal), which is whisky from Scotland. Within that, there are five categories: two "single" varieties and three types of blends. It may seem complicated, but I promise it's easy—watch.

SINGLE MALT SCOTCH WHISKY is made from nothing but malted barley, water, and yeast, at a single distillery. This is your Macallan, your Glenlivet, your Lagavulin. SINGLE GRAIN SCOTCH WHISKY has traditionally been the "filler" in *blended scotch whisky*, often there to lend the drink a lighter flavor. By law, it must be made with some percentage of malted barley, but other grains may be used. BLENDED MALT SCOTCH WHISKIES are, as the name suggests, a blend of two or more *single malt scotch whiskies*. You might know them as Sheep Dip, Monkey Shoulder, or Johnnie Walker Green Label. BLENDED GRAIN WHISKY is a blend of *single grain scotch whiskies*. And finally, BLENDED SCOTCH WHISKY is the most common of the five, and is a blend of either *single malt scotch whisky* or *blended malt scotch whisky* with one or more *single grain scotch whiskies*. Brands include Johnnie Walker Blue Label, Chivas Regal, and Dewar's.

WHAT YOU'RE DRINKING

Then there's American whiskey (the "e" is back, but some producers, such as Maker's Mark, spell it the Scottish way—there's no consistently followed rule). There are a few types of American whiskey. BOURBON WHISKEY is an American whiskey made from at least 51 percent corn. Bourbon doesn't (contrary to popular belief) have to come from Bourbon country or even Kentucky. It can be made anywhere in the United States as long as it follows some rules about how it's made.[2] RYE is another American whiskey, made from at least 51 percent rye, anywhere in the United States. TENNESSEE WHISKEY *does* have to be made in Tennessee, and its rules are nearly identical to bourbon's. In fact, trade law simply states that Tennessee whiskey is a *bourbon whiskey* made in the state of Tennessee.

IRISH WHISKEY has considerably fewer rules than its Scottish and American counterparts, with the law mainly stating that it must be distilled in Ireland and aged in oak casks for a minimum of three years. The majority of Irish whiskies out there are blends, although there are *single malt Irish whiskies* and *pot still Irish whiskies*, the latter of which is made only in a pot still, which lends a richer flavor.

---

2 Other rules of bourbon stipulate that it must be made from at least 51 percent corn, cannot be distilled to more than 160 proof, may not contain any additives, and must be aged for a minimum of two years in new, charred oak barrels. There are many more rules, but these are the most important to know.

Proof

Believe it or not, the vast majority of liquor you enjoy is cut with water before bottling. How much water is added to your booze depends mostly on what type of alcohol it is.

Spirits generally have different ABVs that are somewhat defined by style. So vodka and tequila are usually 80 proof, bourbon is around 90, gin is around 94, bonded whiskey is 100, cask-strength whiskey is around 120, 151-proof rum is exactly 151, all the way up to grain neutral spirit (GNS), available under the brand name Everclear, among others, at 190 proof.

A distiller typically has their preference, which generally skews toward the higher-proof stuff. But the choice to bottle something at a certain percentage of alcohol is almost always done to navigate tax laws, which is kind of sad for us as consumers.

Neat, Up, Straight Up, and On the Rocks

Judging by some extremely awkward drink orders I've received over the years, there seems to be a fair amount of confusion about these terms. I can help.

"Neat" is mainly used for straight spirits. Cocktails generally aren't served "neat," they're served "up." Anything mixed and served in a stemmed cocktail glass would be considered "up."

The notable exception to this rule is the Sazerac, which is most definitely served "neat" in a small rocks glass. Think of it as a term likely invented by a grizzled old cowboy, someone who didn't need a bunch of stuff standing between him and his whiskey. Get it? It's "neat," not "messy."

"Straight up" is where the confusion comes in. It's this sort of catch-all that bleeds between spirits and cocktails. Generally speaking, though, "straight up" means "no ice." You can have a glass of straight tequila, or a margarita served up, but typically never a straight margarita or a tequila up. Yeah, it's kinda confusing that way.

"On the rocks" is easy. I'd like to think that pretty much everyone knows that this means served over ice. "On the rocks" can refer to a spirit or a cocktail. You can drink a vodka on the rocks or you can order a Manhattan on the rocks. Just know that you only need to specify rocks for cocktails that are normally "up," such as a martini.

Adding Ice or Water

There are a lot of people out there with some pretty strong opinions on how you should enjoy your whiskey or other straight spirit, and I honestly have no idea why this is so important to them. It's so pervasive these days that drink writers have tried to coax some similar such opinion out of me on multiple occasions, hoping that I'd lay down the law for whiskey drinkers everywhere with some sort of nonsense about how putting ice or water in whiskey is sacrilege. And those (terrible) drink writers have always been disappointed when I've dropped how I *really* feel about the use of ice or water in whiskey, particularly whiskey that I'm not drinking: I couldn't care less.

There is no rule for when to add water or ice, or to withhold one or the other, from a glass of booze. And anyone who tells you otherwise simply doesn't know what they're talking about. Sometimes I feel like having a whiskey on the rocks. Sometimes I don't. Sometimes I add a small splash of water. Sometimes I add a large splash of water. Sometimes I even add a splash of chilled soda water. There's really no rhyme or reason to it; it's all based on my preference at the time.

And that's the only rule you need to have. It's entirely up to you; if anyone tells you you're doing it wrong, that's just dumb. It doesn't matter, it's nobody's business, and you can drink your whiskey however you like. Now go get 'em, tiger.

The "Back"

When you're enjoying a straight spirit, sometimes it's nice to have something "behind" it, a "back." Think of it as a backing vocal track on a song—it provides a little support to the main event. It's often a small glass of something cold: a soda water, a ginger ale, or a light, crisp beer. You sip it between sips of your drink as a little palate cleanser, which makes for a nice little ritual while you enjoy your spirit.

If you're in a bar, they'll know how to serve your preferred back. Just name the beverage you want as a back, and then add the word "back." Some examples would be "Maker's Mark, Coke back," or "Jameson with a beer back." Don't go into any more detail than that. "I'd like a Siete Leguas reposado and a small glass of soda water over ice with lime on the side, please" is way too much information. Keep it simple.

When I took over the bar at Clyde Common, the previous management was charging for beer backs, and that was the very first thing to go. I come from the older school of thought that believes as long as a back comes from some sort of tap and not a bottle it should always be on the house. It's a courtesy that a bar provides for its sophisticated drinkers who want to sip their spirit with a little something behind it. If you find yourself at a place that charges for backs, adjust your expectations accordingly.

As for what to pair your shot with, that's up to you. I love a little grapefruit soda with my tequila, and there's something about root beer behind a nice amaro that's always appealed to me. But those aren't things that most bars carry. So you might want to save those suggestions for home and stick to whatever the bar has readily available on tap or in the soda gun, because again, no place is going to agree to open a bottle of something just for one back, as they'll hopefully not be charging for it and thus would likely be dumping the remainder of that bottle down the sink.

DRINKING COCKTAILS

The cocktail is one of the United States' major contributions to the culinary arts. Think about the food and drink we all call American: hamburger, pizza, fried chicken, tacos. These all came from other great cultures that immigrated to this country. And sure, people had been mixing up communal bowls of alcohol with fruit juices, sugar, and spices long before the United States was even a country. But the idea of walking into a bar and ordering a single-serving cocktail made just for you—that's a celebration of the individual. And that's distinctly American.

Even Prohibition from 1920 until 1933 couldn't stop the American thirst for a great cocktail. Many of the classics we still order today come from the years when alcohol was illegal and supposedly difficult to find. But sadly, the other side effect of Prohibition was that we lost many of our great cocktailing traditions and replaced them with binge drinking.

Cocktails became less about craft and quality in the 1950s and 1960s, and the resurgence of drinking in the 1970s only drove the nail further in the coffin with its sickly sweet concoctions and plethora of artificial ingredients. By the 1980s, the desire for a healthier way of life had nearly done away with everything but the vodka martini.

In the 1990s, however, the seeds for a cocktail renaissance were being planted. The new generation of drinkers was obsessed with swing music, the Rat Pack, and classic cocktails. I was one of those bartenders who was slinging every flavor of "-tini" across the bartop while the *Swingers* soundtrack blared from the jukebox.

If it hadn't been for those days, we might not be experiencing today's return to cocktails made by craftspeople who care about quality. These days, it's quickly becoming the norm to see freshly squeezed juices, handmade bitters and syrups, and a dizzying collection of spirits and liqueurs at even the seemingly most mundane bars. I can even get a pretty decent drink at the airport now.

But navigating this new world of cocktails can be intimidating to those who aren't entrenched in cocktail knowledge. What follows is my attempt at demystifying what cocktails are really all about.

Cocktail Basics

As I have explained to so many bartenders I've trained over the years, there are three things, of equal value, that make a great cocktail—good ingredients, a good recipe, and good technique. Having any one of these out of balance results in a drink that will never be as good as it could be.

This gets pretty important when we start talking about ordering drinks in a bar. Is that gin and tonic going to be a whole lot better made with Bombay Sapphire instead of whatever they're pouring by default (also known as "well" or "rail" liquor)? Yeah, definitely. But is it going to be worth the extra price if the ice isn't as cold as it could be, the tonic water is flat, or the lime is brown? No, not really. Treating good liquor badly doesn't make for a great cocktail any more than overcooking free-range chicken makes for a delicious dinner.

Dilution

Try this little experiment sometime: Take 2½ oz of gin and ½ oz of dry vermouth, pour them into a martini glass, and then put the whole thing in the freezer. After an hour, take out the glass, drop in an olive, and take a sip. It's horrible, right?

You can't make cocktails that way any more than you can take a whole chicken, some red wine, stalks of celery, unpeeled carrots, and a whole onion, throw it in the oven, and hope that it turns into coq au vin. Cocktails need to actually be prepared, and if you want to make a cocktail that people want to drink, you've got to either stir or shake it with ice, because cocktails are a certain percentage of water.

Shaking and Stirring

One of the most common questions I'm asked when I'm behind the bar is, "How do you know when you should shake a cocktail and how do you know when to stir?" From afar it looks like there isn't much rhyme or reason to it. But of course there is.

What you're doing when you shake or stir a cocktail is simple: you're chilling and you're diluting. You need the drink to be cold, and of course you need the drink to be watered down a touch, but you also need the ingredients to be combined and homogenous.

The general rule for shaking or stirring is simple. We shake drinks that are cloudy, meaning they contain anything like fruit juice, cream, or egg whites. A margarita is a perfect example of a cloudy drink. So is a Tom Collins and a Ramos Gin Fizz. But we stir drinks we consider to be "clear," or that don't contain anything other than alcohol, such as a martini or a Manhattan.

Shaking a drink "wakes it up," and that violent shaking introduces hundreds of tiny air bubbles, and those bubbles dance on the tongue of the person who is sipping the drink. Stirring a drink is a much gentler way to combine and chill and doesn't come with any air bubbles. Stirring leaves the cocktail denser than shaking does. Shaken drinks are light, refreshing, and fun. Stirred drinks are rich and contemplative.

Some bartenders will tell you that you need to follow these rules about shaking and stirring to the letter, and I agree for the most part. If a drink contains juice or fruit purée or fickle ingredients, such as eggs or dairy that don't ordinarily combine well with

others, then you should always, always shake it. I can't think
of any exceptions to this rule. But I don't think the reverse is
true. If you like the flavor and texture of a shaken martini, then
by all means do that. I even prefer my Negronis shaken quickly
before being strained over fresh ice. Those bold flavors can take
a little lightening up. Is it a crime to shake a Manhattan? Not at
all. Just do yourself a favor and don't stir your egg white whiskey
sour. (Gag.)

Bruising Gin

You're going to read an occasional opinion on the horrors of
shaking gin, that somehow jostling the spirit in a small metal tin
with some ice cubes will irreparably damage the gin in such a
dramatic way that you can taste this new, bruised flavor in your
martini.

And I'm here to tell you that this is 94-proof bullshit. Gin is
shipped in cargo containers over rough seas, for weeks. It is
then placed on trains and in trucks that bump the liquid around
mercilessly until it arrives at your liquor store. If gin, or any
spirit, was really so fragile that it couldn't take a shake, we
would have billions of dollars of unusable bruised gin on our
shelves at any given time.

Think about it for a second. Even cheese doesn't bruise when
you drop it on the floor. Some of what's commonly accepted as
fact these days has to have started life as a joke, most likely

made by someone with a liver of steel who didn't want their gin overly diluted by shaking a martini.

So take it from me—you can't bruise gin. Ever. It's not a real thing, so don't let anyone tell you otherwise. Feel free to shake.

Egg Whites

Maybe you've noticed that bartenders are putting egg whites in just about everything these days. Where on Earth does this come from? Why is everyone suddenly using them in everything? Are you going to get sick from drinking these cocktails?

The use of egg whites in cocktails dates back to the nineteenth century, when sugar was far less refined than it is today. Bartenders often used egg whites as a clarifying agent when making simple syrup, which would coagulate with impurities in the syrup and could then be skimmed out, producing a crystal-clear simple syrup.

One can easily imagine that bartenders quickly figured out that egg whites left in the syrup or added to the drink left the cocktail with a rich, silky mouthfeel. Egg whites in cocktails, sours in particular, became very popular in the late 1800s and early 1900s. Sadly, after Prohibition we lost many of those little tricks, which were then rediscovered by bartenders nearly a century later—and now egg white cocktails are very much back in vogue.

I think a lot of modern bartenders tend to go overboard on the egg whites. If the original rationale of using them was to give the drink a rich, creamy mouthfeel, then serving a drink with a three-inch head seems a little out of control to me. I personally don't want my drink overpowered by egg, which does come with a certain . . . eggy flavor. I lightly beat my egg whites before use and measure out a mere tablespoon per drink—that's plenty.

As far as getting sick is concerned, yeah, it's definitely possible but fairly unlikely. People who are sick, have compromised immune systems, are pregnant, or are small children should avoid raw eggs entirely. But then again, those of you who fall into one or more of those categories might want to avoid alcohol altogether anyway.

The rest of us should practice safe food handling. Statistically, you will avoid salmonella about as much as you'll avoid being struck by lightning.

Recipes

One question I get asked all the time is, "How do bartenders remember all of those recipes?" It's much, much simpler than you might think. See, most cocktails are members of just a handful of basic cocktail "families." Gary Regan did a very thorough job outlining pretty much all of them in his groundbreaking book, *The Joy of Mixology.* But to simplify things even further, here are the main cocktail families you need to know, from which you can make 90 percent of the drinks out there.

The HIGHBALL FAMILY are the red-headed stepchildren of cocktails. They garner little to no respect among cocktail snobs, save for the gin and tonic. And to be fair, they are generally little more than an alcohol-delivery system, designed to get the booze in your belly with little to no effort. Screwdrivers, whiskey Cokes, vodka sodas—they're all essentially the same drink. Highballs should all be generally the same proportion, a ratio of 2:3, spirit to mixer.

The OLD-FASHIONED family is one of the most basic cocktail families out there. At its core, it's little more than a spirit touched with a tiny bit of sugar, with a little accent for flavor. A mint julep is basically an old-fashioned with an accent flavor from fresh mint. In the case of the Sazerac, that accent is Peychaud's bitters and absinthe.

The MARTINI family is a catchall I use to describe any drink that consists of a base spirit and vermouth or some other fortified wine, often with bitters added. Obviously the martini falls under this umbrella, as does the Manhattan, Vesper, Vieux Carré, and so on.

The SOUR family is one of my favorites. It's just a base spirit, some form of citrus, and a sweetener. Most of the drinks we enjoy are sours. From the whiskey sour and Tom Collins to the cosmopolitan, daiquiri, and mai tai.

Straws

Some people get real weird about straws. Some drinkers—men, mostly—take it as a personal affront when you place a straw in their drink, as if you just handed them a gin and tonic in a baby bottle. And some drinkers seem to instinctively reach for a straw as a crutch—they'd never dream of consuming alcohol without the use of a straw.

It's personal preference, of course, but I have my own rules regarding straws.

I only use one straw per drink. I think two seems excessive and is usually just a subtle trick bars use to get you to finish your drink more quickly so that you buy another one.

I never use a straw for anything served in a short glass or a stemmed glass, with one exception—blended drinks. These always get a straw and a wide (or "turbo") straw at that. This is the exception to the stemmed-glass rule. Of course, I'll take that blended strawberry daiquiri you just served me in a giant brandy snifter (the only type of drink that one should use that glass for) with a straw. And tall drinks, such as a Tom Collins, always get a straw. Without one, they're too awkward to drink without spilling on yourself.

Ice

While it's terrible wordplay, there's still no other way to say it: ice is very hot right now. Bartenders are obsessed, drinkers are intrigued, and nearly everyone seems to be under some sort of spell when it comes to the very simple phenomenon of freezing water and putting it in a drink.

Let's face it, ice is nothing more than water in its solid form, and it's solid because it's below 32°F. And despite all of the scientific speculation we have to sort through when discussing ice, the rules are actually quite simple: your ice should be as cold as humanly possible, or as cold as your freezer gets,[3] and larger ice or ice with less surface area melts less quickly than smaller ice or ice with more surface area. Outside of that, there's not much to it.

Spherical ice is very popular right now because a sphere has the least amount of surface area of any three-dimensional object, which means that it melts more slowly than, say, a cube. But honestly, how long does it take you to enjoy a sip of whiskey? Is procuring an ice ball really worth it? Because whenever I have a drink with an ice sphere in it, I feel like I'm in the opening scene of *Raiders of the Lost Ark* and that giant boulder is rolling toward Indiana Jones, only it's coming straight at my face.

---

3 Yeah, not all ice is 32°F, in fact, most of it is colder. 32°F is just the freezing point of water, not the temperature of all ice.

Clear ice is cool. It looks cool, and it sorta melts a little more slowly because it's denser. Most ice, like the stuff in your freezer isn't clear because it freezes from all sides at once, trapping naturally occurring air bubbles inside the ice. People tell you to boil the water first to prevent that from happening; they're wrong. Others tell you to double boil it; they're wrong, too. Some folks recommend putting a small insulated cooler full of water in your freezer, claiming that the directional freezing forces the air bubbles to the bottom. This is the correct answer, but who on Earth wants a cooler taking up the entire freezer?

There are these things called "whiskey stones" out there: you pop them in the freezer and then put the cold stones in your drink. Voila, no melting, just ice-cold whiskey. So why not just put the whole bottle in the freezer? A little dilution is the whole point of popping an ice cube in your spirit, right?

And at the end of the day, these sad workarounds are what we're left with when we don't follow those two simple guidelines for making ice that works best in spirits and cocktails: It should be as cold as possible and as large as you can get it. Outside of that, they're all minor differences.

03.

WHEN YOU'RE DRINKING

Possibly the most important times to raise a glass out there are special occasions. Those moments when we put the work aside and pause our normal responsibilities are meant for drinking. Who could imagine their best friend's wedding, a bachelor party, or the Super Bowl without a drink in hand?

Drinks pair well with moments of meaning, importance, and value, which means they're the perfect accessory for important moments in life. Weddings are toasted with Champagne. Sloshy mugs of cold beer are crashed together when teams score touchdowns. Glasses of whiskey are raised when promotions are given. It's just how we do things.

DRINKING HOURLY AND SEASONALLY

I'm a firm believer in the idea that certain drinks are best served at different times—and that certain times are best served by different drinks. While telling people when and where they're allowed to enjoy certain drinks just feels wrong in many ways, I think you've also got to admit that without some rules in place, it's just pure chaos out there.

So while I don't want to refer to these ideas as rules, at the same time, I do want to impress upon you that they're strong suggestions. See, the fun in having rules is that we get to break them. And when we break a rule, especially when it's a nonessential rule like when we're allowed to have certain drinks, we feel a little naughty and it feels fun.

In general, you don't order a Bloody Mary after noon. If you need to, you can stretch the time limit to say that you can order one within two hours of waking up. So, say you're in Vegas and you just happen to wake up at two in the afternoon (I, of course, don't know what you're talking about), then you can safely order a Bloody Mary by four PM and be fine. But once the sun goes down, you can't drink a Bloody Mary in public. Only men with lower-back tattoos do that.

Spirit-driven cocktails should be reserved, in most cases, for after the sun sets. Two exceptions would be a martini at lunch and a Negroni in the afternoon. But you never have a Manhattan with breakfast. Breakfast isn't Manhattan time (see "Drinking at Breakfast," following).

Drinks should get stiffer only as the day progresses. What this means is that you don't *have* to order stronger and stronger drinks as the day goes on, but you don't start your day off with an old-fashioned. You can always go back, but you never skip ahead. Like, it's fine to have a mimosa at midnight, but drinking a martini at breakfast is a move that only an alcoholic makes.

The most fun rule to break is that summer drinks must be consumed in the summertime. Ordering a strawberry daiquiri in the dead of winter, when it feels like you haven't seen the sun in a million years, is one of life's great pleasures. But it's a guilty pleasure; we don't chug piña coladas all winter long.

Once the temperature rises above a certain point, though, you have to stop ordering hot drinks. Having a nice warm green Chartreuse and hot chocolate in the lodge after a day of skiing is a pro move. Drinking an Irish Coffee on the Fourth of July is an amateur move.

Drinking at Breakfast

There aren't a ton of super-appropriate drinks that go with breakfast. Sure, there's the mimosa, the Bloody Mary, and pretty much any sort of coffee drink. And one other you're probably forgetting: the Ramos Gin Fizz (page 58).

The scourge of day bartenders everywhere, the Ramos Gin Fizz is easily one of the most complicated drinks in history. Even the drink's creator, Henry Ramos, of New Orleans, employed a small army of assistants to help execute the popular drink for his clamoring crowd. But you and I don't have time for that nonsense.

I don't order them when I'm out, because I know I'm just going to irritate the bartender and, quite frankly, most bartenders don't make good ones. But at home you could be known for whipping up a legendary Ramos at breakfast. And it couldn't be easier when you own a blender.

Blending a drink with one large (1 by 1-inch) ice cube is an old bartender's trick. And being an old bartender, I use it more often than not. It's easier than shaking, it produces better results than shaking does, and the cleanup is a hell of a lot easier.

Drinking at Brunch

Occasionally you're going to find yourself in a position of hosting a Bloody Mary brunch at your place. And you should. Maybe there's a game on, maybe it's a baby shower, whatever. It's one of the skills any host should have. I hate to say it, but there are some technical difficulties associated with making a Bloody Mary. I mean, in some ways, it's a very simple drink, but in

ramos gin fizz

3 oz London dry gin

1 oz freshly squeezed lemon juice

1 oz freshly squeezed lime juice

1½ oz Rich Simple Syrup (page 127)

3 oz half-and-half

1 egg white

6 drops orange-blossom water (available online and at most specialty grocers)

2 large ice cubes

2 oz club soda or sparkling mineral water, chilled

makes 2 cocktails

Here's how you throw together a couple of Ramos fizzes in no time at all.

Place two Collins glasses in the freezer to chill.

In a blender, combine the gin, lemon and lime juices, simple syrup, half-and-half, egg white, and orange blossom water with two large ice cubes. Blend until you no longer hear the ice cubes rattling around in there. Split the club soda or mineral water between the chilled Collins glasses and then pour the blended mixture on top of each. Serve with a straw.

other ways it brings up a lot of issues when you're talking about making a bunch of them for a crowd.

The first thing is that it's kind of time consuming. I mean, if you want to do it right, you really have to take some time. There are a lot of ingredients that have to go in there, you've got to measure out the vodka and tomato juice, and then you still have to mix and garnish the whole thing. Do you really want to make thirty of those? Even I don't want to do that, and it's way easier for me to do it than it is for you.

The second problem is that using a mix just sucks, period. You're probably using a mix from the grocery store, which I guarantee is always, always horrible, no matter how fancy the label, no matter how many buzzwords they slap on there about it being homemade or small batch or organic. Store-bought Bloody Mary mix will always suck. So, what—do you make your own mix then, and just let people add vodka to it? Definitely don't do that either. Because what's going to happen is you're either going to run out or you're going to be left with a bunch left over, which you will then end up pouring down the sink. You will never, ever have exactly the right amount of Bloody Mary mix. That's a fact.

So at work, we came up with this pretty awesome little trick to help speed up brunch service, while still avoiding that second issue. We combine everything that goes into a Bloody Mary, with the exception of the vodka and tomato juice, and use that as a sort of base (see page 61) upon which we can add the other ingredients.

But here's the really great thing about this base: it's super flexible. Someone in the group wants theirs extra spicy? Throw a couple extra dashes of hot sauce in theirs. Someone wants a Bloody Maria, made with tequila? Glad you didn't pre-mix the vodka, right? Have a bunch of Canadians over, and they want Caesars? Add Clamato instead of tomato juice. Don't finish the whole bottle of pre-mix? That's cool, this thing's got enough salt and acidity in it to last for weeks in the fridge!

Drinking at Lunch

I'm not really one for day-drinking. I don't know why. Maybe I just have too much to do or maybe I just start wondering what the hell I'm doing with my life once I catch that midday buzz. But when I do—and it's rare, believe me—I always try to do it with style. And that's why I'm a big fan of what I call the European café cocktail.

bloody mary pre-mix

12 oz freshly squeezed lemon juice

12 oz Worcestershire sauce

1½ tsp finely ground black pepper

1½ tsp celery salt

1 tsp Tabasco or Crystal hot sauce

makes enough for 24 servings

Whatever you do, don't let anyone tell you that a Bloody Mary is better with freshly puréed tomatoes—it's not. In fact, it's super gross. Tomato juice is made from roasted tomatoes, not fresh-off-the vine tomatoes. Roasted tomato juice is sweet, full of flavor, and rich. Fresh tomato juice is foamy and vegetal and tastes like crap.

To make a Bloody Mary, all you have to do is combine 1 oz of this mix with 2 oz vodka and 4 oz tomato juice, add ice, garnish with your choice of pickled vegetables, and serve.

In a pitcher, mix together the lemon juice, Worcestershire, pepper, celery salt, and hot sauce. You'll end up with an amount that fits in a 750 ml bottle, so if you have an old wine or vodka bottle lying around, you can just pour the pre-mix in there and refrigerate for up to 3 weeks.

The café cocktail is the perfect beverage for day-drinking: it's refreshing, low in alcohol, and perfectly suited to pairing with food. It is built from three components and so well tailored to the mix-and-match approach. The first is a bitter component; this is usually in the form of some sort of Italian liqueur such as Campari, Aperol, or Cynar. The second piece is a type of wine; sometimes it's just plain old wine, sometimes it's sparkling wine, or sometimes it's fortified wine such as vermouth, Lillet, or Dubonnet. And the third is a sparkling element like sparkling water or sparkling wine.

You can throw these three things together over ice, garnish with a lemon or orange peel, and voilà!—you have a café cocktail. Campari, sweet vermouth, and sparkling water? You've got an Americano. Aperol, prosecco, and sparkling water? It's an Aperol Spritz. Campari, dry white wine, and sparkling water? That's a Bicicleta. And Campari, sweet vermouth, and prosecco? It's called a Negroni Sbagliato.

Drinking at Dinner

I'm going to be ostracized by the vast community of cocktail nerds for saying this, but with very few exceptions, I don't believe in cocktail pairings with dinner. And I'll probably get a lot of emails or comments showing every single example of cocktails that work well with food, but whatever. I'm kind of a traditional guy in this regard. I believe in the classic dinner progression. I start my evening with a classic cocktail, a dry martini perhaps. In the winter I like to switch it up to a Manhattan. In the summer I might make it a Negroni.

When it's time for food, I switch to wine. There are a few reasons for this. Wine is a lot more delicate than cocktails or spirits. Wine doesn't overpower food; it complements it. Wine is, usually, considerably less strong than cocktails. I've never been able to wrap my head around the "three-martini lunch." How did anyone get any work done back then? Anyway, when dinner is just about over, and it's time for dessert, I like to end the night with a neat spirit or a final cocktail. When I'm having Italian food, maybe it's grappa or amaro with an espresso on the side. When I'm at my favorite steakhouse, I might finish with bourbon or Islay scotch.

But, hey, not every meal is a sit-down six-course masterpiece. A couple of margaritas will never not be enjoyable with a plate of tacos. Ever. Big, sweet, tiki-style drinks actually work really, really well with spicy Asian food. But for the love of Christmas, putting down six old-fashioneds with dinner is not what a sophisticated drinker does. You're not just having wine with dinner, you're also signaling to your dinner companions that you're not a total pig. Drink accordingly.

Drinking to Birthdays

Ask any bartender—and I mean that—go ask any bartender, maybe in the world but definitely in the United States, and they will all tell you the same thing: It is a myth that bars are supposed to give you a free drink on your birthday.

I have this sneaking suspicion that the whole thing started with Denny's back in the early 1990s, when the diner chain ran a very famous promotion (of which a more modest version still exists today) where they announced, in radio and TV spots, "We're buying everyone in America a meal on their birthday."

And as brilliant of a marketing scheme as it was, I think it sort of bled over into other areas of the service industry. I can't even begin to tell you how many times over the last quarter century I have watched people stride right up to the bar, with full confidence, and demand their free birthday drink. Total strangers. Not even regular guests.

So if you're going out on your birthday, and you're hoping for a free drink, feel free to ask if the house offers any birthday specials. But don't leave your wallet at home because, at many places, the most you're going to get is a warm and sincere "Happy Birthday" as the bartender hands you the tab. And if you're out with someone whose birthday it happens to be, don't ask. All of their drinks *are* free—because you're paying for them.

Drinking to Holidays

If you're not drinking on a holiday, you're doing something wrong.
I mean, that's kinda what holidays are for, am I right? Whether
it's margaritas on a dock somewhere warm on Labor Day or
putting down mug after mug of spiced toddy at Christmas in an
effort to dull the pain of time spent with certain family members,
drinking on a holiday is just what we do.

There are two types of holiday we drink to. First, there are the real holidays. You know, Mother's Day and Christmas, and other occasions like that. But then there are the drinking holidays. You know, the ones you don't get to take time off of work for: Cinco de Drinko, Mardi Gras, and so on. Drinking holidays are the worst. I think they make a lot of sense when you're in college, but staying out all night on St. Patrick's Day when you're over the age of thirty is just . . . the thought of it makes me sad.

That said, you need some tips from a survivor of many, many holidays, on both sides of the bar.

NEW YEAR'S DAY (January 1) calls for leftover Champagne and orange juice at home. Sure, a Bloody Mary is a popular choice, but in all likelihood, you've got to work the next morning. Do you really want to wrap up the holidays with even more vodka? Personally, I want something a lot softer to ease me back into the real world.

I make sure I've got plenty of inexpensive Spanish cava and fresh oranges or high-quality orange juice on hand the day before, since most of the stores are going to be closed. And who wants to put on shoes anyway? New Year's Day should be spent in sweatpants with movies, mimosas, and comfort food. The year officially starts tomorrow.

VALENTINE'S DAY (February 14) is, of course, a great occasion to book a romantic table for two at a super-nice restaurant. But it's an even better occasion to learn how to shuck oysters, perfect the Dry Gin Martini, and not get stuck listening to someone else's

dry gin martini

2¼ oz London dry gin[1]

½ oz dry vermouth

1 cocktail olive, or wide twist of lemon peel, removed with a vegetable peeler

makes 1 cocktail

When I first started making cocktails, no drink in the world freaked me out more than the martini. I'd get these really awful older men sitting in front of me judging my martini "skills" while I worked. Now I know the truth: A martini is a very basic two-ingredient cocktail. Nothing could be less intimidating.

I've tried just about every ratio of gin to vermouth and the 5:1 gin-to-vermouth ratio is the one that's the most appealing to the widest audience. You can adjust the recipe to your own personal taste. Anyone you serve this recipe to is going to love it. And it also happens to be my favorite. Hint, hint.

Place a cocktail glass in the freezer to chill. In a mixing glass, stir the gin and vermouth with ice. Strain into the chilled cocktail glass. Garnish with the olive or my personal favorite, the lemon twist, and serve.

1 Some good friends of mine make this stuff called Ford's Gin—if you can find it where you live, it's the perfect martini gin.

idea of romantic music. You can go out tomorrow night. And trust me on this one: making cocktails at home for someone is super, super sexy. Even my bartender's cold heart skips a beat when someone makes me a cocktail at home.

MARDI GRAS (forty-seven days before Easter Sunday) is one of the all-time great amateur drinking holidays. Any time you trade your dignity for a plastic beaded necklace, you know you're deep in amateur drinking territory.

Fans of getting sick on Hurricanes all night will try to tell you that they're in some way honoring the rich history of New Orleans by binge drinking at a sports bar and harassing women to take their shirts off. But New Orleans is so much more than Bourbon Street, and on Mardi Gras, I like to tip my glass to the Crescent City by preparing a perfect Sazerac, made with equal parts Kentucky rye whiskey and estate-grown cognac. No beads.

ST. PATRICK'S DAY (March 17) teaches us that nothing says layman drinker like donning a bunch of really ugly bright-green bullshit, strapping on a little plastic top hat, heading down to P.J. McNasty's, and drinking Irish Car Bombs until you're barfing creamy tan foam when the sun comes up on March 18.

Look, skip the Irish Car Bomb, okay? The name is really offensive, and quite frankly it doesn't even taste that good. If you're at a bar, ask to see what Irish whiskies they carry that might not be the usual two you've ever ordered. Try a single malt Irish, a pure pot-still Irish, or even a rare peated Irish whiskey. And if you're feeling only mildly adventurous, why not try to perfect the Irish Coffee at home? One part Rich Simple Syrup (page 127) to three parts Irish whiskey and six parts hot coffee is a good place to start.

SUNDAY SPRING HOLIDAYS Easter (Sunday, after the first full moon that falls on or after the vernal equinox), Mother's Day (second Sunday in May), and Father's Day (third Sunday in June) are generally day-drinking events. Never let the drinking during one of these occasions carry on through the evening. The drinking is over once the sun goes down. Your mom doesn't need to see you wasted on her special day, so keep it under control.

I don't think there are necessarily cocktails associated with any of these dates, but I will say this: I have never, ever found a perfectly made mint julep to be the wrong call on any of these days. I also really like sours and Collinses on Sunday holidays, but a nice big bowl of punch is also a lot of fun for a spring gathering.

WHEN YOU'RE DRINKING

Father's Day also coincides with the finals of the U.S. Open Championship, so if your dad's a golf fan, a nice bottle of scotch is probably in order. If not, maybe just slip some vodka into an Arnold Palmer and call it good.

CINCO DE MAYO (May 5) is not Mexico's independence day. It commemorates the Mexican victory over the French at the Battle of Pueblo in 1862 and is not even widely celebrated in Mexico. I'm not saying it's not fun as hell. I love tequila and I love margaritas, Mexican beer, and Mexican food. But I'm a grown-ass man, and the idea of binge drinking tequila poppers at a Mexican chain restaurant on a Tuesday night is really troubling to me.

Tequila is an agricultural product, so for the love of all that is holy, please throw some support at small, independent tequila producers who make a quality spirit. The big brands will be just fine without your business, but the people who are working hard to maintain the traditional methods of harvesting, fermentation, and distillation really need your support. So whether you're drinking at home or at the bar, find a tequila that you can feel good about ordering.

MEMORIAL DAY WEEKEND (the weekend adjacent to the last Monday in May) is, for many, the unofficial beginning of summer. This is that crucial moment when you want to pick your summer drink. Picking a new drink for summer is a time-honored tradition, and you should have been thinking about it well in advance of Memorial Day. Try out a few if you need to. Take them for a spin this weekend and announce your summer drink once you've got it all figured out.

Here are a few starter suggestions. A cucumber daiquiri is easy, just muddle a few slices of cucumber in the bottom of a cocktail shaker and build a daiquiri right on top of it. Blended Negronis are really fun; just throw a Negroni in a blender with the juice of 1 orange, 1½ Tbsp of Rich Simple Syrup (page 127), and a scoop of ice. Have you had a Radler (half lager, half grapefruit soda)? Iced Keoke Coffees might even be the best thing yet—coffee, cream, crème de cacao, and Kahlua over ice? Sounds like heaven to me.

FOURTH OF JULY (July 4), American Independence Day, is a gauntlet of day-drinking that often trails well into the night. Make sure you've got a plan for avoiding total blackout by the time the fireworks start. My main defenses are low-alcohol punches, a cooler full of various flavored sodas (I like to mix it up, throw some Jarritos flavors in there, and whatever else I can find at the local Latin supermarket), and lots and lots of food. Fortunately, the latter is covered at any standard Fourth of July barbecue. And once the fireworks are over, have a nightcap on the porch with friends and call it a night. You've got work in the morning, champ.

LABOR DAY WEEKEND (the weekend adjacent to the first Monday in September) is typically the end of summer. So it's your last chance to enjoy your official summer drinks, and then you've got to start thinking about holiday cocktails. The weather is about to turn and you can't still be drinking raspberry margaritas in October. You're an educated drinker now; you can't be caught looking like an amateur.

Hit your local homebrew shop and pick up some supplies: some 6 or 12 oz glass bottles, a bag of bottle caps, and a bottle capper, oh, and a funnel if you don't already have one. The whole setup will cost you under thirty bucks. Now, make a big batch of your favorite summer drink and fill as many of those empty bottles as you want. Cap them with the bottle capper, pack them in a cooler full of ice, and bust them out at whatever Labor Day event you've been invited to.

HALLOWEEN (October 31), and autumn in general, is all about apple cider. So I always gravitate toward apple drinks. Warm wassail, cold apple cider punches, and simple rum-and-cider or bourbon-and-cider highballs are my kind of drinks. I'll make my own, or even better, I like to take a long autumnal drive out to a farm that produces their own fresh-pressed apple cider. I'll pick up a gallon and host a little Sunday dinner party with cold apple cider cocktails.

THANKSGIVING (fourth Thursday in November) drinking is a real test of stamina. If you are the cook, you may start in the morning provided that you are eating the entire time. If you are not cooking, you help the cook, you provide drinks (you could make the cider punch on page 74), and you surreptitiously watch to ensure the cook doesn't peak too early. This is important. Nobody gets drunk on Thanksgiving, they just get really, really tired.

REPEAL DAY (December 5) is one you might not have heard of, but you should have. One slow night at work back in 2001, a regular was sitting at the bar reading the paper. He noticed

thanksgiving cider punch

1 (750 ml) bottle rye whiskey

1 qt fresh apple cider

1 cup freshly squeezed lemon juice

1 cup Rich Simple Syrup (page 127)

3 oz Fernet Branca

1 tsp Angostura bitters

15 cinnamon sticks

15 twists orange peel

makes 15 (5 oz) servings

If I've got a big group coming over, there's only one thing to do: pop a big batch of hot apple cider cocktails in the slow cooker, set out some teacups or coffee mugs, and let everyone ladle up their own.

In the insert of a slow cooker (never on a stove with an open flame), combine the whiskey, apple cider, lemon juice, simple syrup, Fernet Branca, and bitters. Cover and heat on the medium setting. Serve in mugs and garnish with the cinnamon sticks and orange twists.

the "On This Day in History" section and remarked that on that day back in 1933, Prohibition was repealed. It got me thinking: Why don't bartenders celebrate Repeal Day as a sort of revered holiday? Without Repeal Day, I, for one, would be working in an architecture firm instead of doing what I really love.

So the following year, I rounded up a group of bartenders, and we went carousing at all of our favorite watering holes. I printed up a little card with some information about Repeal Day, as we were now calling it, and urged all the local bartenders and drinkers to celebrate with us.

A few years later, I posted something about Repeal Day on my cocktail blog and urged people everywhere to join me in celebrating it, particularly those who were into more refined cocktails than, say, the St. Patrick's and Cinco de Mayo drinkers. And sure enough, that started something in the cocktail community. Within a very short time, bars everywhere, not even just bars in the United States were celebrating Repeal Day.

Now Repeal Day is kind of an accepted occasion. It falls right between Thanksgiving and Christmas yet isn't a family-oriented holiday, and it's easy to celebrate: no special costumes or specific nationality's drinks to limit yourself to. I still suggest that everyone exercise their constitutional freedom and enjoy at least one drink on Repeal Day. As I said in that original blog post: Simply celebrate the day by stopping by your local bar, tavern, saloon, winery, distillery, or brewhouse and having a drink. Pick up a six-pack on your way home from work. Split a bottle of wine with a loved one. Buy a shot for a stranger. Do it just because you can.

HANUKKAH (date based on the Hebrew calendar) should be spared Manischewitz at all costs. Come on. There are plenty of wonderful kosher beers, wines, and spirits on the market. Clear Creek Distillery in Portland, Oregon, produces a kirschwasser (cherry brandy) and slivovitz (blue plum brandy) that are both certified kosher. Seek them out.

CHRISTMAS EVE/CHRISTMAS (December 24/25) drinking is one of the most important and least addressed traditions of Christmas. Christmas drinking requires fortitude. You will be tested by travel. You will be tested by weather. You will be tested by relatives. And yet you may not get so drunk that you air your decades-old grievances with your brother-in-law. You know what kind of drunk you are (sentimental, loving, judgmental, or angry). Drink accordingly.

One reason egg nog is such a great holiday drink is that everyone is going to get full before they have a chance to reveal what kind

clyde common eggnog

4 large eggs

¼ cup superfine or baker's sugar

4 oz añejo tequila

5 oz amontillado sherry

12 oz whole milk

8 oz heavy cream

1 whole nutmeg

makes 8 (5 oz) servings

This is the version we serve during the holidays at Clyde Common, one of my bars in Portland, Oregon. It's made with añejo tequila and amontillado sherry. It sounds weird at first, but the combination tastes like nog made with bittersweet chocolate and roasted hazelnuts.

Place small cups in the freezer to chill.

In a blender or stand mixer fitted with a paddle or whisk attachment on low speed, blend the eggs until smooth. With the blender running, slowly add the sugar until it is completely incorporated and has dissolved, and then slowly add the tequila, sherry, milk, and cream. Transfer to punch bowl, cover, and refrigerate until cold. Serve in the chilled cups. Dust with freshly grated nutmeg before serving.

of drunk they are. There's no way to have too much egg nog, unless you've got the stomach of a Viking.

NEW YEAR'S EVE (December 31) is an important night to be somewhat drunk, because the real holiday is New Year's Day, which is to be spent nursing your hangover and finishing the leftover Champagne.

But New Year's Eve is tough, isn't it? I'm somewhat glad that most of the New Year's evenings I've spent were behind the bar. Because, honestly, there's so much pressure to do the "perfect" thing at midnight. So you crawl around from crappy house party to crappy house party or spend way too much money so you can be at a club. And it's never what you want it to be, is it?

So if I'm not working, or I'm not entertaining at home for New Year's Eve, my plan is this: Go out for a really nice dinner somewhere, and start late. Dinner at eight-thirty is this wonderful, luxurious thing (and rare in the West). Anyway, I get dressed to the nines, have some cocktails, have dinner with some wine, and then I find the funnest, diviest, dirtiest bar near to where I'm staying and drink really bad martinis, stay overdressed, until midnight. And next year, I'll do it all over again.

DRINKING TO HOLY MATRIMONY

Marriage ceremonies and alcohol have been inextricably linked since the dawn of time. Back in the day, the parents of a Chinese bride would offer wine to the parents of the groom to formalize their acceptance of the union. The father of the bride typically offers the first toast at modern weddings. And the word "honeymoon" is reputed to be derived from the first month (or "moon") after a wedding, when a couple would consume mead (a sort of wine made from fermented honey) and, well, mate. Yeah, I don't like that word either.

Many of these ancient traditions have fallen by the wayside, which is fine. I know that when I end up tying the knot, I certainly won't be able to take a month off work, and I don't actually like the taste of mead all that much. But alcohol does play an important part in the traditions leading up to a wedding (who *hasn't* met their significant other in a bar?). I attended a booze-free reception once—I didn't stay long. And thus opens a whole world of fun possibilities where spirits and cocktails come into play.

Bachelor/Bachelorette Parties

Having a bachelor party is like having a bachelor's degree: at the time, you think you're pretty special, but when it's all over you realize that (a) everyone has one, (b) you don't remember half of it, and (c) you made some very questionable choices while you were doing it. So with that in mind, why not just skip over it and go straight for the master's?

STEP ONE: Pick a location. You wouldn't think that this part has anything to do with alcohol, but OF COURSE IT DOES. Do you want to go somewhere that has drinks available for purchase, like Las Vegas or Manhattan? Or do you want to hunker down somewhere and drink your own booze, like you would at a house on the beach that you've rented for the weekend? Both have pretty strong plusses and minuses, so no matter what you choose, adjust your drinking plans accordingly.

STEP TWO: Pick an activity. The activity is an important part of the stag or hen party, and it's generally a time—maybe the only time—that you're not actually drinking. You know, you're at a day spa or going horseback riding or taking a race-car driving class, that kind of stuff. Unless you're actively touring wineries, breweries, or distilleries, you're engaging in something mildly physical. Put the booze down for a few hours.

STEP THREE: Pick a dinner. Okay, now you can start drinking. If you're the best man or maid of honor, this is your time to shine. You should have already selected a special bottle of something, and your time to present it to the group is now, before you have dinner. When my best friend from high school got married, I pulled out a twenty-one-year Balvenie I'd been saving just for this occasion. Reveal the bottle, give a little information to the group about why it's special to you, and drink at least half of it before you go to dinner. Don't forget the toast.

STEP FOUR: Drink. Here we go. And look, this is a master's degree we're talking about. Ladies, if you're even considering walking up and down Broadway in Nashville, or the Strip in Vegas, covered in plastic penises and getting throw-up drunk, you need to get your ass back in school. Fellas, if blowing a thousand dollars at the sleaziest strip club in town is what you've got planned, that's bush-league stuff. Find the best bar in the city and start with one single round there. Then take it down a notch. Move on to someplace loud and fun. Keep it to a minimum, because the goal here is to make it to the end of the night.

For your last drink, you should be huddled together drinking straight spirits at the coolest dive bar in the world. There should be a jukebox—a real one, not an internet one—and you should all be telling war stories and congratulating the bride or groom while offering sage life advice. That's how it's done.

flasked old fashioned

4 oz bourbon or rye (bonus points for something high-proof)

1 oz water

½ oz Rich Simple Syrup (page 127)

4 dashes Angostura bitters

4 orange peels

makes 3 or 4 servings

This recipe will fit in a common 6 oz flask, the sort you are likely to carry to a wedding.

In a 1 qt measuring glass, combine the bourbon, water, simple syrup, and bitters. Squeeze the oils from the orange peels over the mix and discard. Using a funnel, pour the mixture directly into a 6 oz flask. Store the flask in a freezer or on ice until ready to serve.

Flasks

If you are in the wedding party, you must carry a flask. There are a number of slim, compact, discrete flasks available on the market. Every discerning drinker should not only have at least one (personally, I have more flasks than I know what to do with), but also have strong opinions about flasks in general.

The flask you bring to a wedding is for the bride or groom—it is not for you to get drunk on. Think of it as a sort of first-aid kit. Getting up in front of all of your friends and family and pledging your life to another person for eternity has got to be a little nerve wracking, I would imagine. I don't know for sure. But a little nip of booze is probably a decent way to relax a little before you go up there. I do know that every single person I've handed a flask to before a wedding has been extremely grateful. The flask is for these sorts of emergencies only.

If you're the best man or maid of honor, it must be expensive or special. You can fill the flask with something crazy, like a really expensive spirit, or something rare from your collection. It can be the recipient's very favorite spirit. It can have some special significance to the two of you from your younger days. But it's never something you just grabbed because it was cheap and readily available. Make it special.

Still, straight alcohol can be a little off-putting to some people, so whipping up a stiff little cocktail to carry in your flask and slipping it in the freezer or setting it on ice until it's time to head to the altar isn't a bad idea.

Champagne Pyramids

My brother-in-law, Joe, is one of the best bartenders I know. Well, he used to be, anyway. Now he's more of a family man with a real job, but back in the day I learned a lot from him about drinks and drinking. And I learned more about throwing a party the day he married my sister than just about any day prior or since.

I had totally forgotten about the time-honored tradition of the Champagne Pyramid until Joe revived it for me on that day in August. And I'm so glad that he did, because I've been building them ever since, always to great response. There are few things more impressive to a party full of people than a cascading tower of bubbles.

The Champagne Pyramid is a striking piece of architecture— and I'm a sucker for architecture. If you're unfamiliar with the concept, allow me to explain: a literal "pyramid" of Champagne saucers (or coupes) is constructed at a party. Bottle after bottle of Champagne is poured into the top-most glass, which then overflows and cascades down, slowly filling every glass in the pyramid with Champagne.

WHEN YOU'RE DRINKING

It's an impressive spectacle to witness, and when the show is over, everyone can dismantle the pyramid and toast with a full glass of Champagne. Here's how you construct your own.

I always begin with a 13 by 18-inch rimmed baking sheet. Mine at home are often fairly banged up, so this is usually a good time for me to spend the ten bucks and pick up a brand-new one at the restaurant supply store (rimmed baking sheets are great for everything, from using as serving trays to laying out parts when taking apart a computer). A new one is good to have because your base needs to be perfectly flat.

The baking sheet is also important because it will catch the spillover, and the last thing you want to do when throwing a party is spend fifteen minutes clearing everyone out of the room so that you can mop a bunch of wine off the floor.

I also grab a case of Champagne coupes at the restaurant supply place while I'm there. They're cheap, you can use them for cocktails as well as Champagne, and they're pretty durable. I get the Libbey 5.5 oz Embassy Champagne Coupes. A case of 36 will make a sizable tower for 30 people.

Okay. Now that you've got the goods (and hopefully you've picked up enough Champagne or sparkling wine by now), start by placing the baking sheet on a level surface. Level is important if you want all of the glasses to fill at the same rate. Anyway, I start with a 4 by 4 grid of glasses (so, 16 glasses) in the center of the baking sheet. Be as anal as you can about getting those glasses lined up perfectly; it's going to make for a much more impressive show later on.

Centered directly on top of your 4 by 4 grid, build a 3 by 3 grid (9 glasses). Remember, be as precise as you possibly can. On top of that, you guessed it, set up a 2 by 2 grid (4 glasses). And at the top, dead center of that perfect pyramid, put one single Champagne saucer.

Now the fun begins. You're going to slowly pour bottle after bottle of Champagne into that top glass while your gathered guests watch the bubbles slowly cascade down the pyramid, filling each layer of Champagne saucers until moving on to the next. Soon, every glass will be full and you can hand the topmost glass to the guest of honor and let everyone take their own.

Baby Showers

Hey, you know what? Baby showers sometimes don't have alcohol. And that's totally fine. You can be okay with this, you don't need to bitch and complain to everyone about it, and you don't need to run to the nearest convenience store for a bottle of Blossom Peak or whatever, you lush.

Here's what you do instead: Look like a nonalcoholic baby-shower rock star. First, hit the nearest thrift store—St. Vincent de Paul, Goodwill, Salvation Army, whatever. Inside, in the housewares section, they are 100 percent guaranteed to have a punch bowl and as many punch glasses as you need. Pick out your favorite set and take it home and wash it; thrift stores are gross.

On your way to the baby shower, stop by the grocery store. A big, cheap, chain grocery store is going to be better for this next step than some sort of high-end gourmet grocer. You need to pick up just four things: sherbet, juice, soda, and berries. When you get to the party, hit the kitchen and throw all of those ingredients in the punch bowl, mix it up well, and serve it. And, see, now you look like a hero. Congratulations.

sherbet punch

½ gal your-choice-flavor sherbet

1 qt fruit juice (orange or pineapple are usually what I grab)

1 (2 L) bottle of 7-Up, Sprite, Sierra Mist, or ginger ale

1 cup fresh or frozen berries

makes 32 (5 oz) servings

There's really no wrong recipe here. It's sherbet punch. It's not supposed to be some thought-provoking cocktail. It's supposed to be fun and campy and silly and celebratory and nonalcoholic.

___

In a punch bowl, combine the sherbet, juice, and soda and stir to dissolve the sherbet. Add the berries and serve.

04.

WHERE YOU'RE DRINKING

Sure, we all drink at the bar, and we drink at home. And in restaurants, and sometimes at work (let's just pray that we're not doing all this on the same day).

There is an elegance to drinking in bars, when you're out at a restaurant, at home, at work, etcetera, that sometimes goes missing in this day and age. And now that this sort of drinking renaissance is upon us, it's a good time to discuss the best ways to go about drinking in different situations.

Because how we drink is just as important as what we drink.

DRINKING IN A BAR

Let's face it, most of the time that you're drinking spirits and cocktails, it's going to be in a bar. Bars are great places to learn about the hard stuff, for a couple of reasons. First, it's a hell of a lot cheaper to try a cocktail at a bar than it is to stock your home bar with all of the necessary ingredients. Sure, cocktails seem kind of expensive, especially when you compare it to the actual value of the drink. But when you really think about it, what's ten bucks for something that would cost you a hundred to make at home?

The other reason bars are great places to learn about spirits and cocktails is that you've got experts there to help you. They get paid to know more than anyone else about this kind of stuff, so take advantage of the fact that you're there.

Getting Service at the Bar

There's no shortage of diatribes written by cranky bartenders who are tired of adults who never quite figured out how to order a drink in a bar without abandoning all manners and immediately declining into some real knuckle-dragging caveman behavior.

And that's a shame on both counts, because it's really, really easy to get a drink in a bar.

When you approach the bar to order a drink, pick a location and wait patiently. That's all you have to do! The bartender knows exactly who is next and will be with you as soon as they can. Waving your hands, shaking a fistful of money or flashing a gold card, calling out to the staff, or trying to order from the barback[1] is unacceptable, and it doesn't get you a drink any more quickly. Rather, it only irritates the staff. And let's face it, do we really want to spend time at a bar where the people working are irritated by our behavior?

Take it from a guy who still works behind the bar full-time, and has done so for well over twenty years. Bartenders do this work because it's fun. We get to take care of people, we get to make new friends from all over the world, and we get to make people happy. And we are pretty good at what we do. So when you walk in the door, we know you're there! Waving your hands in our faces or snapping your fingers at us turns this fun job that we enjoy into little more than an unpleasant business transaction.

So just hang out in one place, wait patiently, and we'll be right with you, even if we're too busy to tell you so. A busy bartender is the sign of a great bartender. It means the bartender is working

---

1 The barback's job is to assist the bartenders. A good barback either never makes eye contact with you or informs you that one of the bartenders will be right with you. Shouting drink orders at them as they run past you will accomplish nothing.

even harder for you, not less. And hey, if you find yourself in a bar where the bartender doesn't seem to care and is just standing around, just find another place to drink. They obviously don't need you there keeping them from doing nothing.

Where to Sit

When bartenders get busy, everyone in the bar or restaurant starts to look the same. So when some folks get up from a table or bar and you immediately sit down at said dirty table—or bar seat—without us seeing it happen, we often think you're the same person who was there before. Sitting there and then becoming increasingly frustrated that nobody has come to take your order isn't doing anyone a favor. Neither is stacking everything up at the edge of the table or bar.

So, perfect the art of the hover. Stand near the seats you wish to occupy, and I guarantee that someone will rush right over; whisk away any leftover glasses, plates, or utensils; and get your evening started.

Getting Table Service in a Bar

There are two types of bar: those that provide table service and those that don't. If you're going to sit at a table, and the establishment hasn't bothered to make it very clear how the process works, then you're going to have to do some recon.

Hover at the table for a second before you sit down. Did someone rush over to greet you? No? Well then you'd better have a seat. This might take a while.

Does it seem like there are cocktail servers working the floor? Then you can assume they'll be right with you. Flagging down every person who walks by your table in an apron is not necessary. Again, the staff knows you're there. Relax a bit, talk to your friends, and wait patiently for someone to get over to you. Catch the cocktail server's eye if you must, and I promise they'll get to you as soon as they can. If you're in a massive hurry, maybe you should be drinking at home.

If it's pushing five minutes, make a move for the bar. The bartender is probably happy to take your order (and your money) if you're sitting at a table. You're obviously willing to do half the work by getting up and walking over to the bar, so you're likely going to make someone happy.

But sometimes we happen upon a place where they just don't do their job well. Either the staff doesn't care, or they're simply not trained to succeed. And so, if you've waited for an unreasonable amount of time without so much as being greeted by anyone, to be very honest with you, I would probably just get up and leave. The place is either too busy, or they just suck at their job. So without making a scene or saying a word, I'll simply walk out the door before I even have a chance to order. There's someone else out there more deserving of your time and money.

Calling "Placebacks"

A napkin or coaster placed over a drink is an indication that the drinker will be right back. You may not sit in their seat, not even for a second, not even to order a quick drink, not even if the place is crowded. They arrived before you, and their space is sacred.

I've seen more conflicts take place in bars because someone simply didn't understand this basic concept. Just imagine how confusing and inappropriate it would be if someone helped themselves to your airplane seat while you were in the restroom or sat with your date at dinner while you had excused yourself for a couple of minutes to take a phone call. It just doesn't make sense.

So if you see that someone has temporarily given up their seat at the bar, stand behind the empty seat and wait for the bartender. I guarantee that being twelve inches closer to the bartender isn't going to get you a drink faster. In fact, the bartender is probably watching out for their seated guests, so show some deference and they might even get to you faster since you already seem like a pleasant and patient person.

Selecting Your Drink

I get it. Sometimes even I get so overwhelmed by the options available to me these days that I draw a blank when I'm asked for my drink order. It's like filling out the "Hobbies and Activities" section on a dating website, walking into a giant record shop, or visiting the New York Public Library. Suddenly I can't remember what I enjoy doing; I have no idea what sort of music I like and no recollection of any single book I've ever heard of.

One night I stepped into a friend's busy bar after work and was so flustered when he called out to me across the busy room that I just shouted back "gin and Coke!" It was like the record skipped and everyone in the room was judging me while my bartender friend just shook his head and frowned at me.

So before you start to square up to the bar, it's good to have some idea of what you'd like. Asking the bartender, "What's good?" or "What should I have?" is not a drink order. You can build a drink order out of parameters, like, "I'd like something with tequila, on the sour side, and served up," but do know that this tack isn't going to work someplace that doesn't do a lot of cocktails.

These are drink orders:

"I'd like something low-alcohol and refreshing."

"I usually drink Maker's Mark, neat. Is there another bourbon I might enjoy?"

"I need something strong made with gin."

"Can you recommend something hot/cold/sparkling/bitter?"

These are *not* drink orders:

"What's good?"

"What do you make well?"

"What should I have?"

"What do you feel like making?"

"I'll have whatever that person over there is having."

To make life easier on myself, I have a drink that I order in every specific type of bar. It's my method of coaxing the best possible drink out of wherever I happen to be by decreasing the probability that someone will be able to screw it up.

If I'm in a DIVE BAR, NEIGHBORHOOD BAR, or LOCAL BURGER JOINT and I really want a delicious cocktail, I order a bourbon and cranberry juice. Yes, I know it sounds a little unorthodox, but that's partly why I like it. It's different, yet it can be made in any bar in the world. It's simple, but it's pretty complex-tasting for a two-ingredient cocktail; the sweetness of the bourbon works well with the tartness of the cranberry juice. If they've got a wedge of lemon handy, I'll usually take a squeeze, but not lime. Bourbon and lime aren't great bedfellows.

My vacation drink for when I'm at a RESORT or POOLSIDE BAR is Myers's rum and orange juice. It's strong, it's tropical, it's different, and it's one of the few drinks that isn't horrible with prepackaged juice. Now, sure, I'm always game to try the establishment's version of a mai tai or piña colada, but nine times out of ten I end up going back to that dark Jamaican rum and orange juice. Seriously, try it sometime.

When I find myself at a RESTAURANT BAR, I usually order a Negroni. The Negroni is a great call because any decent restaurant is going to have the ingredients on hand to make it: gin, sweet vermouth, and Campari. It's literally impossible to screw up the recipe, because it's equal parts of each. And to be honest, there isn't a lot of technical know-how needed to pull it off: it's not ideal, but your bartender could just pour it all into a glass, top with ice, and hand it to you. And it would still be pretty good. It's the most forgiving classic cocktail in the world.

But what about when you're at a FANCY COCKTAIL BAR? Well, I'm of the opinion that you should always order a daiquiri. Why? Because it's the only place that's going to make you a daiquiri the way it should be made. Yeah, sure, it's not going to take advantage of their house-made barrel-aged bitters or whatever, but they'll get over it. And most of us who work in fancy cocktail bars really enjoy and have a lot of respect for the daiquiri.

What to Talk About at the Bar

Drinking is a time for conspiring, sharing secrets, engaging in passionate discourse, agreeing, disagreeing, and, of course, telling people that you love them. But all too often we forget we're out in public when we're many drinks deep at the bar.

Bartenders are taught to not engage in discussions involving politics and religion, because those topics tend to ruin a good time. While we certainly don't want to dissuade you from participating in lively conversation with your friends about such topics, we also have to be vigilant that such conversations don't evolve into physical altercations. So do us, and yourself, a favor and keep it civil. Please.

Using Your Phone at the Bar

Old cranky types just love to embrace the false notion that before smartphones, everyone in the bar sat around and practiced the fine art of conversation, honed their wit, and generally engaged in erudite tête-à-têtes all night long. And as someone who was (ahem) tending bar before cell phones were even widely used, I've got to tell you that these pundits are full of shit.

When I started behind the bar in 1996, we kept a small stack of fresh newspapers near the front door. The guests would fight over the different sections, because even back then people wanted to sit and enjoy a drink in silence without a lot of human interaction. Some people would just stare at the TV, or play the lottery. My point is that smartphones didn't kill the art of conversation. In fact, it's still very much alive, as evidenced by the loud din at my bar every night of the week.

There have been so many pointless diatribes written about how cell phones should be banned from bars, and I've even been in bars where there is a no-cell-phone policy. It's just so silly. Should you be allowed to use your phone to read or text with people when you're sitting by yourself? Of course you should. It's the twenty-first century, and people need to get over it.

Should you have your ringer turned up or be playing music or loud videos on your phone? No, definitely not. Nobody wants to listen to it, so keep your ringer off, and for the love of all that is holy, do not watch videos or play music on your phone without

headphones. That sort of behavior is just begging to have your ass thrown out.

Is it cool to talk on your phone at the bar? Maybe. Just remember that the other guests at the bar don't want to listen to a loud phone conversation any more than they want to listen to a loud in-person conversation at the bar. Be considerate of others and keep it down if you need to talk on the phone. Even better, step away from the other guests or even step outside. This isn't your office.

Can you get them to charge your phone at the bar? You can ask, for sure. But if there's not a convenient outlet, or the bar doesn't have the specific cable for your phone, it's not their problem. It's your responsibility to keep your phone charged, so if the bar can't provide power for you, and it's super important to you, then maybe it's time to head home and plug in your phone.

In short, the rules of using your phone in a bar aren't all that different from the rules of using your phone in any public place: be respectful, be considerate of others, and don't expect the world to revolve around you and your phone. Outside of that, you don't need to feel bad about looking at your phone any more than you should feel bad about reading a book.

Sending Someone a Drink

We've all watched a lot of movies and TV shows and been shown what would be considered some pretty questionable behavior in reality. Real life isn't like the movies, and ushering the bartender over and commanding that a drink be sent over to a complete stranger isn't really mysterious, chivalrous, or elegant. It's just kinda creepy.

Let me go on the record and say this: I think people should be given a pass if they're really young or really old. They haven't gotten the memo yet, and that's okay. In fact, it almost seems cute coming from them. But the rest of us think it's a little weird to have a drink sent over by a secret admirer. In fact, "secret admirer" even sounds a little predatory.

At our bars, if someone insists we send a drink down to the other end of the bar, we'll casually sidle up to the target and ask them if they'd like to accept a drink from someone at the bar. We don't name names or let them know who is doing the asking; there's no point in embarrassing anyone. But we simply approach the situation with a gentle, "Someone at the bar would like to buy you a drink. You don't have to accept it if you don't want to. But if you do, bear in mind that person is probably going to want to talk to you."

And yeah, 99 percent of the time, the answer is a firm "No thanks." At that point we're forced to head back to the poor sap and inform them that the object of their desire isn't there to meet anyone and that the drink has been rejected. Half the time the response is a sad sulk away from the bar. The other half results in, "I wasn't asking permission—just send it anyway," which usually just results in the check delivered and the door shown. We're not in the business of forcing drinks on people.

So if you absolutely need an ice-breaker and want to send a drink over, by all means get your bartender (with whom you've hopefully developed a positive rapport) to ask on your behalf whether the other guest would like a drink sent over. If the answer is no, well then you've saved some face, been respectful, and probably don't look like a huge creep. If the answer is yes, just remember to be polite and respectful when you do go sidling up.

Handing a Stranger a Drink

Rule Number One: Don't.

Hey, look, it was awkward enough when you were trying to send a drink through the bartender. Now you're considering just asking for a drink—a shot, even—and walking it over to someone you don't know at all? No. Absolutely not.

In case nobody told you, that's some very predatory-looking behavior, and hopefully most reasonable sorts have been warned about people who behave like that. Walking up to a stranger, handing them alcohol, and saying, "Drink it" is the sort of thing serial killers do, ya know? Use your words, strike up a conversation, and offer to buy the object of your desire a drink once you're both comfortable.

Befriending the Bartender

You want a game plan for how you can successfully hit on that sexy bartender you've been pining after for the past three weeks? Well, unfortunately you're not going to find it here. Those sorts of articles, offering advice on how much to tip, what drink order will impress, and so on, have been written for years. And I've never quite understood why this energy is always spent on hitting on bartenders. You never see the *Huffington Post* sharing a piece on how to pick up the mailman, nor was I able to find a

Thrillist article on the "Top Ten Ways to Score a Date with Your Dental Hygienist."

I can't tell you how to become friends with a bartender any better than I can tell you how to get an astronaut to hang out at your place on weekends. No guy or gal is going to fall for you just because you ordered some cool whiskey. And I have yet to see a person—bartender or otherwise—who responds favorably to a stranger shouting, "WHAT'S YOUR NAME?" as a way of introducing themselves.

Money doesn't buy friendships either—certainly not good ones, anyway. So if you think that an extra couple of dollars is going to get the bartender to give a complete stranger—a buzzed stranger—his or her phone number and risk exposure to crazy, unwanted text messages and phone calls, you should rethink that.

So here's an idea: if you're truly interested in pursuing a friendship (or more) with the person serving you drinks, why not get to know him or her? Maybe get to know each other in the process? A simple, genuine, and honest conversation with another human being is going to be worth more than all of the whiskey and dollar bills in the world.

Tipping

I don't believe in discussing tipping. It's such a hot-button issue that there's no way to even speak about it without ruffling quite a few feathers. People who already feel disenfranchised by the cost of going out to eat and drink feel that they're being taken advantage of by an antiquated system. And the folks who spend night after night, and year after year doing pretty grueling physical labor, often making little more than minimum wage, believe they should be able to pay their bills.

People have tried doing away with tipping entirely in this country, and passionate diatribes are written regularly from both sides of the bar in favor of and opposition to this

revolutionary idea. But for now, it's the system we have, and that's how it goes.

One thing I should mention is that tipping is something that always comes in the form of money. It sounds crass, but if I didn't feel it was worth mentioning, I wouldn't mention it at all. Sitting at a bar for two hours eating dinner and enjoying cocktails and then paying your tab and leaving drugs as a tip? Definitely not. I've been "tipped" on many, many occasions with marijuana and cocaine, both of which are of absolutely zero value to me.

There's no real rule for how to tip that's going to appeal to everyone, so I think it's important to develop your own style and your own policies on how you tip people. You're under no obligation to tip anyone, but I will say this: I probably spend a lot more time in bars, restaurants, and coffee shops than most people. I tip warmly and generously whenever I can, and while I do so, I treat the people who are taking care of me with genuine love and respect. And wherever I go repeatedly, I'm welcomed warmly and generously by the people I take care of. For me, that feeling is priceless.

Scoring Free Drinks

We all had that buddy in college who never seemed to charge anyone for anything. But now that guy has either moved on to selling junk bonds or he's working at the shadiest bar in town.

The game has changed, and bars are more legitimate than they've ever been before. You're going to have to open up your wallet.

I've never understood why there's always such an expectation of free drinks in bars. Many regular customers assume that when they've spent a certain amount of time or money in a bar, they're entitled to receive compensation. Do they expect the same thing at the grocery store? Is it expected that when they hit the Taco Bell drive-thru a couple times a week they're going to get an extra Crunchwrap Supreme?

The first rule of free drinks is you never talk about free drinks. You want to be treated? I promise you that asking the bartender will result in you paying full price every time. Mentioning free drinks makes a bartender dry up faster than a turkey breast at Thanksgiving.

Here's what criterion we professionals use to determine whether a drink is going to be free: none. It either happens or it doesn't, and while there's no shortage of nightlife writers out there who offer up their advice on scoring free drinks at the club, I'm telling you, they're all full of shit.

Assuming that there's some sort of secret code that will unlock the fountain of free alcohol is ridiculous. So if a free drink does fall in your lap (so to speak), act surprised, express gratitude, and tip like you're Frank Sinatra. It might happen more often.

Getting Cut Off

Sometimes bartenders have to make the uncomfortable and unpopular decision to tell you that you can't have anything more to drink. It sucks, I know. It sucks even more for us. I mean, it's not like we really want to stop taking your money. We also don't want to get into a confrontation. I once cut off an angry good ol' boy, who then told me in a very deliberate and methodical tone that he was going to go home, get his shotgun, and come back and blow my head off.

So yeah, we don't like cutting people off. But we do it because we care. We care about your safety and want you to get home in one piece. We also care about the community we're all a part of, and we want all of them to be safe as well. Think about it: we don't really know what you're capable of, particularly after you leave us. You could step off a curb and get hit by a bus. You could punch a stranger in the face. Or you could get behind the wheel of a car and kill yourself—or someone else.

In the majority of states in the U.S., the people and establishments who serve you alcohol are also subject to what is known as third-party or dram-shop liability. Here's what that scenario looks like for me: You come into my bar and I serve you enough alcohol that you're now visibly intoxicated. You then go out into the world and do some damage. It doesn't even have to be a matter of you drinking and driving—let's say that you go punch someone in the face. Or spray paint a wall. Or accidentally fall down and break a handrail. I am now legally responsible for any damage that you did while drunk, and the victims of your damages have every legal recourse to sue me, personally, for letting you get so drunk that you caused damage or harm.

Can you imagine the consequences of this? Think about all of the mistakes that drunk people make, and now think about all of the bartenders and servers who can be held responsible for those damages. Do you really think that serving you one last screwdriver is as important to the bartender as not being sued?

So when bartenders let you know that they can't serve you any more, take it on the chin. Thank them for caring about you, ask for a glass of water, and let them know if you need any help getting home. Any one of us would be happy to oblige.

DRINKING AT HOME

One of the most positive things to come out of this drinking renaissance is that people are learning how to drink at home again. And despite the fact that much of my livelihood comes from people going out to drink, I'm all for this development. In my profession, the more excited people are about having a drink, the better we all do.

Whether it's a casual night of drinking with friends in the kitchen, throwing elaborate cocktail parties at home, or just having something to sip alone while you quietly contemplate the day, drinking spirits and cocktails at home is pretty awesome.

These days, people are even building impressive home bars and booze collections that rival some of the cocktail bars I've been to. And their home assortments of house-made bitters and tinctures are perfectly suited to their kitchens full of infused olive oils and sourdough starters.

No matter if you're the casual sort or the serious enthusiast, hopefully you're already enjoying, or about to start enjoying, the joy of a proper drink at home.

The Home Bar

I'm living proof that any hack can get paid to write about spirits and cocktails, so that's not lost on me. But somehow there are people out there who are even worse at this than I am, and those people call me several times a year and ask me to weigh in on the same, tired article that wine, beer, and spirits writers have been trotting out year after year since the dawn of time: What Ten Bottles Should Everyone Stock at Home?

It seems like a pretty simple request on the surface. You want to stock a home bar that maximizes the number of drinks you can offer people while spending the least amount of money possible. Right? 'Cause this stuff gets real expensive, real fast. So, okay, you need this bottle of gin, you have to have this Islay whisky, there's this rum that works in the most number of tropical drinks, and so on.

But I always throw this question back at people who want me to make their shopping list: do you really want some stranger to tell you what you should be drinking at home? If you really don't like gin, does it make sense that I should be telling you to spend your money on a bottle of Tanqueray? A lot of people don't care for the flavor of smoky scotch, so why even bother picking up a whole bottle of this thing that's a super-acquired taste on the off chance you're eventually going to like it?

My advice is this: decide on two or three drinks you really enjoy drinking at home and pick up the ingredients for those. Do you enjoy only vodka drinks? Well, I'm probably not going to suggest you grab a bottle of Fernet Branca. Get yourself a few different vodkas, maybe some liqueurs that you like mixing them with, such as Cointreau or Chambord, and go from there.

But, please, when you read about some supposed authority telling you that you absolutely can't have a home bar without some esoteric bottle that you have no interest in owning, pay no attention to what they're saying.

Basic Bar Tools

There are also bartenders out there who will tell you that you need a ton of really fancy gold-plated equipment to make drinks at home. Believe me, that stuff is really, really nice. I have a whole collection of shiny bar tools, vintage bar tools, and all sorts of other things I've collected over the years. And without fail, I end up using the same few utilitarian items whenever I want to make a drink at home.

So here's a list of the stuff I use in my home bar. If I tell you that you need something, and it's kind of expensive, there's definitely a reason for it. But if there's no need to spend the money, I won't let you. I promise.

ICE: If you don't have an ice machine built into your freezer, then you'll need some sort of tray. I like the 1 by 1-inch silicone molds made by Tovolo. I keep three of them in my freezer at all times, refilling them as I go. Two is a good number and will provide you

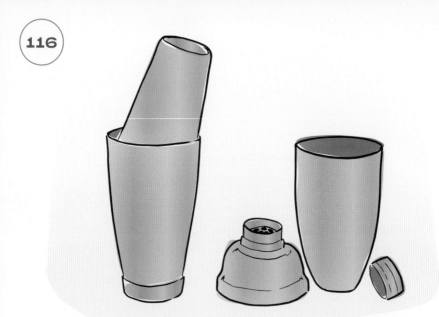

with enough ice for a few drinks before dinner and some rocks for straight spirits after dinner. If you're having a large party or need more drinks than that, you'll need to pick up some bag ice anyway (for more about stocking ice, see page 126).

COCKTAIL SHAKER: At home and at the bar, I use what's called a Boston shaker, which is a two-piece shaker. I use the same pint glass I keep in the freezer for serving beer. They're about a buck each and they're multipurpose. The stainless-steel part, known as a Boston shaker tin, will run you about ten bucks for a good one—the heavier its weight, the better.

STRAINERS: I use the Hawthorne strainer by Oxo Good Grips at home and in both my bars, and a simple inexpensive tea strainer to fine-strain the pulp or other solids out of shaken cocktails. Together they'll run you less than fifteen bucks.

CUTTING BOARD AND KNIFE: If you don't already have some sort of cutting board and knife in your kitchen, I'm wondering how on Earth you manage to feed yourself. Go get a cutting board and knife if you don't have either. You can do a lot with an offset-handled serrated bread knife from the nearest restaurant supply store.

PEELER: Making citrus twists is a hell of a lot easier with a vegetable peeler. Get the y-shaped peeler made by Oxo. Those straight-handled ones are for long vegetables, like carrots. The y-handled peeler is designed for spherical objects like potatoes, or lemons.

BARSPOON: Although I own dozens of really fancy spoons of every size and shape, the implement I reach for most often when I need to stir a cocktail is a plastic chopstick from the local Asian market. It's cheaper than a fancy spoon, it's easier to use, and I don't know about you, but I like eating pretty much everything with chopsticks. I always have a bunch on hand and I almost exclusively stir cocktails with one.

JIGGER: You don't need a fancy-ass silver-plated jigger, I promise. The five-dollar clear-plastic model by Oxo does the job better than most. It's what I use at home. It has both Imperial and metric measurements clearly marked, which is cool if metric is your thing like it is mine. It's also got a little spout on it, which makes it not only easy to use for cocktails, but also pretty perfect for doling out oil for a vinaigrette.

SQUEEZE BOTTLES: I pick up a six-pack of plastic foodservice squeeze bottles on Amazon or at the restaurant supply store every couple of years for about ten dollars. I use them for storing simple syrup and juices for making cocktails and for ice water for serving absinthe.

JUICER: You don't need to spend $150 on a professional juicer for home. I use my $30 Norpro stainless-steel hand-juice press more often than I use anything else. Just give it a quick rinse and towel dry after you use it; putting it in the dishwasher is going to decrease its life expectancy.

BLENDER: Any bartender is going to tell you that you need a $500 blender. I love my Wolf blender, but if you're not using it every day, you don't need to spend the money. However, when you do make blended drinks, you're going to want to buy or make crushed ice (a clean pillowcase and rolling pin can make quick work of a bag of ice) since the motor in those household models isn't strong enough to chew through cubed ice.

I've used enough vacation rentals to know that while having a professional-grade blender is great for everyday use, with the right technique[2] you can coax some pretty stellar piña coladas out of an inexpensive home blender.

---

2 Throw your drink in the blender and start blending on low speed without ice. As you slowly add crushed ice, increase the speed until you're running on high and the drink has a soft, pillowy look to it with crisp folds in the surface as the blender is running.

Buying Liquor

I rarely spend more than $30 on a bottle of booze, and usually half of that if I'm buying wine. In nearly every single category of spirit, there are some really incredible finds for under thirty bucks.

Most specialty-bottle-shop employees are invested in helping you find something interesting. And don't be shy about how much you want to spend: most of the time, they don't care. I know folks are often really shy about asking me for some bargain booze recommendations, but what most people don't know is that finding hidden gems in an affordable price range is one of my favorite things to do! Store employees don't tend to be filthy rich themselves, and if anyone does give you grief about not shopping for a $250 bottle, go someplace else.

But sometimes there's just nobody on hand to help at all. So here are some really oversimplified rules of thumb for when you find yourself at the store.

BOURBON: I have always found the whiskies made by the Heaven Hill distillery to be the most flavorful and least expensive of all the wonderful bourbons out there. They make a ton of products, but most of them don't say "Heaven Hill" anywhere on the bottle, so look for something that says "Bardstown, Kentucky" on the label.

Furthermore, you should take advantage of the U.S. government's bonded whiskey program. That's something of a holdover from a time when trustworthy whiskey producers could separate themselves from disreputable ones by enrolling in a government program that certified their products to be verified and "bonded" at four years old and 100 proof. Though this program is no longer really necessary, those whiskies are still around, they're inexpensive, and they're almost always really, really good.

RUM: I like really flavorful rum and don't typically get a lot of enjoyment out of those overly "smooth" rums from Puerto Rico and St. Croix. Instead, I look for affordable bottles from places like Jamaica, Guyana, Trinidad, and Martinique. Even if all you'll be doing is mixing these with Coke, you're still going to be having a better drink.

I feel like rum should be this fiery, rough, wild spirit from the Caribbean. The sort of thing that pirates drank. So I like my rum to have a little wildness about it. If I need something "smooth," I'll just drink vodka.

VODKA: Super-cheap vodka is, generally, not good. At all. And super-expensive vodka is, generally, not worth the price. So I stay in that middle range with some really well-made and affordable vodkas. Stoli and Absolut have both always been, and hopefully will always be, terrific products. Also, I really like good old Smirnoff vodka a lot. There's a bottle of the 100 proof in my freezer at all times, just for emergencies.

GIN: The best gins are those old-school labels that have been doing it for 150 years. Names like Gordon's, Boodles, Tanqueray, Bombay, and Beefeater have always been the gold standard for London dry gin.

TEQUILA: Tequila is tough. The really good stuff is pretty expensive, and the really cheap stuff is barely even tequila. So here are some guidelines. First, don't buy anything with the word "Gold" on the label; it's not worth your time, it's not tequila, and quite frankly it's got a lot of sugarcane in it. If it doesn't say "100% Agave" somewhere on the label, just skip right over it until you find something that does.

Also, many distilleries make more than one product, and often they make a different price point than their primary or flagship brand. For instance, Herradura makes a less-expensive tequila called El Jimador and it's fantastic. Jose Cuervo makes a higher-end tequila called Centenario that's quite good as well.

You can see a list of everything that's made by a tequila distillery by going to www.tequila.net/nom-database.html and typing in the NOM[3] number. It'll bring up a list of every product made at that same distillery. Try it with some of your favorites and see what other tequilas they produce.

Simple Syrup

If you're going to get serious about making drinks at home, you should get in the habit of maintaining a bottle of simple syrup in the fridge at all times. I'm never without this magic sweetener. I use it for everything from coffee in the morning to old-fashioneds before dinner.

One of the bummers about plain old sugar is that it doesn't dissolve super well in cold beverages. That's why, when you add spoonful after spoonful of sugar to your iced tea, you're always just left with a sad lump of undissolved sugar at the bottom of the glass. It also doesn't dissolve super well in alcohol, which is

---

3 Norma Oficial Mexicana (NOM) is the government-regulated tequila distillery number found on every label.

why an old-fashioned made with a sugar cube always has those little sugar granules at the bottom of the glass.

The way bartenders get around this is by pre-dissolving the sugar in water, making a syrup that will easily dissolve into just about anything. There are, of course, many different types and recipes out there, but the all-purpose simple syrup that lives in my fridge is a basic Rich Simple Syrup (two parts sugar to one part water, page 127) made with everyday white granulated cane sugar.

I use plain old white sugar because it comes with a neutral flavor that works in everything. And I make mine in the rich ratio because all of my cocktail recipes are tailored to that ratio, and it lasts longer in the fridge than syrups made with less sugar.

Making Cocktails at Home

Nobody, and I mean nobody, is expecting you to be a master mixologist at home with a fully stocked bar, awaiting orders to fill. My home is more well-stocked than most small bars are, but when I'm entertaining, I'm not at work; I'm there to spend time with my guests.

el diablo

1½ oz silver tequila

¾ oz freshly squeezed lime juice

½ oz Rich Simple Syrup (page 127)

½ oz crème de cassis (black currant liqueur, or you can substitute Chambord in a pinch)

2 oz ginger beer

1 lime wedge

makes 1 cocktail

The El Diablo was one of the first cocktails I mastered at home, and if you ever came to a party at my house back in the late '90s, I more than likely fixed you one at some point. It's not your typical tequila drink, which is why I like serving it at home; it's a little something special that people will surely remember.

Place a Collins glass in the freezer to chill.

In a cocktail shaker, combine the tequila, lime juice, simple syrup, and crème de cassis. Shake with ice cubes until cold, and then add the ginger beer. Strain over fresh ice cubes into the chilled Collins glass. Garnish with the lime wedge.

You should know how to make one cocktail at home, perfectly. Become famous in your circle of friends for this drink. Pick one and master it. You will be a hero. If you're not going to say, "Tonight I will be making my world-famous El Diablos for everyone," then you should provide a basic bar and let people make what they want. But there's not much fun in that.

Nonalcoholic Beverages

We, as hosts, should always provide nonalcoholic beverages for people. You don't have to provide a million of them, just a few staples. Soda water. Coke, etcetera. Some are even disguised as mixers. Because the difference between a good party and a great party is in the details.

Making flavored simple syrup is one way to keep an ingredient on hand that can be used to make interesting drinks, both alcoholic and nonalcoholic. I start with the Rich Simple Syrup recipe (page 127), and then add dried spices and let it infuse over a period of anywhere from an hour to up to a day, depending on how hardy the spice is. Then it's just a matter of straining out the solids, bottling, and refrigerating. Simple syrup that is infused with dried spices rather than fresh spices lasts much longer.

Here are some suggestions of spices that infuse really well into the Rich Simple Syrup recipe while it's still hot.

DRIED THYME: 1 tbsp, steeped for 15 minutes

LAVENDER (ORGANIC): ¼ cup, steeped for 30 minutes

PINK PEPPERCORNS: 2 tbsp, crushed, steeped for 4 hours

VANILLA BEAN: 2 whole beans, split, steeped overnight

Stocking Ice

You may think that you're stocking enough ice for a party, but you're not. Do you ever wonder why even the simplest of drinks always taste better in a bar than they do at home? One of the biggest reasons is because we use enough ice. Not stocking enough ice for a party, and not using enough ice in drinks are probably the most common mistakes I see people make when serving drinks at home.

In a professional bar setting, glasses get filled to the top with ice. Always. This isn't done because we're trying to stiff you on booze. It's done because you want to be able to enjoy a cold drink, whether you realize it's what you want or not.

We never use the same ice more than once at the bar, either. If I shake a margarita for you and serve it on the rocks, the drink gets shaken, and then strained over fresh ice. It's subtle, but it means the difference between a decent drink and a great drink.

rich simple syrup

16 oz granulated sugar

8 oz water

makes 12 oz

You can measure your sugar and water by volume (two cups of sugar to one cup of water works), but for the most accuracy, I like to measure by weight. A digital scale is cheap and super useful for all sorts of kitchen projects. I strongly recommend you pick one up.

In a small saucepan or microwave-safe bowl, combine the sugar and water and give it a good stir. Heat until the sugar is just dissolved and then remove from the heat. Set aside to cool. Transfer to plastic squeeze bottles (see page 118) and refrigerate for up to 2 weeks.

flavored sparkling lemonade

1½ oz freshly squeezed lemon juice

1 oz infused simple syrup (see "Nonalcoholic Beverages," page 125)

4 oz chilled sparkling water

1 lemon wedge, sprig fresh herb, or whole vanilla bean

makes 1 serving

I love flavored sparkling lemonades pretty much all the time. And sure, they're great nonalcoholic beverages, but you can also get away with adding vodka, gin, or even silver tequila to any of these.

Combine the lemon juice, simple syrup, and sparkling water in a tall glass and fill with ice. Garnish with the lemon wedge, herb sprig, or vanilla bean.

Get four times as much ice as you think you need. Put it in a cooler, in the freezer, or in a sink if you must. But never, ever run out of ice. And keep in mind that a single margarita can use close to a pound of ice.

Feeding People

Are you having people over to drink? Give them food. I can't tell you how many dinner parties I've been to where everyone is falling down drunk before the salad even hits the table. People don't need anything fancy. Ritz crackers and a can of dip make most people happy. Lipton Onion Soup Mix, a tub of sour cream, and a bag of chips. There you go.

There is a reason there are always hors d'oeuvres recipes in the back of old cocktail books: because cocktail parties used to be cool until people forgot how to make a lousy cheese dip. Eventually, getting blackout drunk at someone's house stops sounding like a good idea.

Drinking at Home, Alone

Drinking at home by yourself is one of life's great pleasures, and one of the best parts about being an adult. Sure, it's a joy to do with friends, but it's a fine thing to do alone from time to time. And believe me, sometimes you must. A hot toddy by the fire with a good book—or a sultry old-fashioned after a long day at work—it doesn't matter. A little solo drinking, in your own castle, is often called for.

Sometimes it's a good time to think without the distraction of other people. The ritual of preparing a drink, slowly stirring a martini, or polishing that special crystal tumbler you only use when you're drinking the good stuff, is important.

Do not finish a bottle of whiskey all by yourself. This is time for contemplation, not for texting your ex. There's a not-so-fine line between having a quiet contemplative drink and just getting wasted at home by yourself. Stay on this side of sobriety. Nobody likes a drunk shut-in.

Drinking in the Bathtub

One of my regulars at the first bar I worked in was named Gene. He was in his mid-forties and hung out with the large group of regulars who congregated every night to watch *Wheel of Fortune* and catch up over a few beers. Sadly, Gene was an alcoholic.

Gene usually kept it real at the bar, but he'd almost always buy a six-pack at the end of the night before heading home. One night he had one too many, slipped in the shower, and hit his head. He suffered a brain aneurysm and died shortly thereafter.

I'm all about a beer in the shower or a glass of wine or whiskey in the bathtub. But you've got to be careful, and mixing a lot of alcohol with slippery wet surfaces is a really bad idea. We all loved Gene very much, and it was hard for us to come to terms with losing someone we cared about to something as simple as that. Please be careful.

DRINKING AT SOMEBODY ELSE'S HOUSE

There is an art to being a good guest. Think about every time you've hosted a party: there are guests you enjoy having over more than others. Don't get angry at me for pointing this out. They're *your* lousy friends. Every host knows who the good guest is going to be, and they look forward to their arrival. Be that guest.

Coasters

Coasters are such a weird invention. I mean, I've been dealing with coasters for forty hours a week for the past two decades, and I still don't really understand what they're all about. I mean, I know that their primary intent is to prevent condensation rings on surfaces, but who really cares? And why are they so prevalent in bars if that's the case?

First of all, who uses a coaster at home? I certainly don't. My dining room table is an old oak library table, so it can withstand a lot of abuse and has also developed a really nice patina over the past fifty years. My coffee table has a glass top, so I'm not worried about that. And my kitchen countertops are marble, so a little condensation ring isn't going to ruin that.

Have we finally moved past the era when people owned these fragile, precious tables that required a coaster? My parents own a really formal dining room set, but who has a formal dining room anymore?

At the bar, this logic doesn't make any sense. No bar is ever going to be made of a surface that can be damaged by water rings, believe me. Bar tops are some of the most durable things in the world. Do you really think a little water is going to harm one? For me, I think the bar coaster is more about providing you with a soft little landing spot for your drink. Banging your glass on a bare bar can be somewhat jarring. So a coaster is a nice little pad.

And at a bar, you're primarily sitting in one spot. At home, you're moving around quite a bit, aren't you? That's why I think coasters are kind of silly at home, and make sense in a bar. But remember this: if you're at someone's house and they insist that you use a coaster, you must oblige. Don't argue, just use a coaster.

BYOB

The acronym "BYOB" was created by people with shitty friends as a way to remind them of the most basic rule for attending a party: always show up with a bottle of something. To be honest, it makes me a little sad that I even have to write this. But it's true, and somehow there are people out there who never got the memo.

If you've been invited to a party, you bring a bottle. Most of the time, you show up with wine. If it's a cocktail party, you bring a bottle of liquor. And if it's a barbecue or the party is during the day, you bring beer. Are there exceptions to these rules? Sure. Is not bringing something one of the exceptions? Nope.

You never ask for the bottle you brought to be opened, and you don't take it home if it didn't get opened. Got it? Once you walk through that doorway, the bottle officially belongs to the host. If you want to drink what you brought, bring more than one.

There are really only two benefits to hosting a party at your house: first, you don't have to figure out how to get home after the party is over and, second, you end up with some bottles at the end of the night. That's it. The rest of it is cleaning.

Broken Glass

Here's the problem with glassware: it's made out of glass. And after nearly a quarter century of working with the stuff, I can tell you that eventually, it's going to break. Things made of glass are ephemeral, temporary, a fleeting moment in time, soon to be only a memory. This is why you don't see a lot of glassware in museums. It's all been broken by people who were drinking.

On that note, if you're having a party and someone breaks one of yours, you should remember this: it's not a big deal. So grab a broom, sweep it up, and assuage their stress when they invariably apologize profusely. Did that glass cost you a lot of money? Because you can purchase them at a thrift store for 50 cents a piece. You know this, right? Was this some precious antique that has been in your family for a hundred years? Well, that was dumb. Now you have three, and a reminder not to use them when company comes over. Move on.

On the flip side, if you break a glass at someone else's house, you should pretend to be apologetic. It's only polite to pretend to care, even though you and I both know that it's only a glass. Offer to clean it up, apologize three times, and then move on. If your friend is going to try to make you feel bad for breaking a lousy glass, you don't need that kind of negativity in your life. Cut your losses and move on. You'll find new friends eventually.

There is, of course, a right way and a wrong way to clean up broken glass. Sweep up what you can and get those broken shards into the recycling—no bare hands! You also don't put broken glass into a trash can with a plastic liner, because someone it going to cut their leg open taking it out to the trash. Put those big shards in the recycling bin with the other glass.

But you still need to wipe up the slivers, those barely visible little shards that are going to get into every finger and toe you have. And when it comes to wiping up, there's one cardinal rule you must follow: no cloth. Use a paper towel or disposable wipe; otherwise, once that cloth hits the washing machine, you're going to be discovering broken glass slivers in everything you own: underwear, pillowcases, towels . . . you get the point.

Cleaning Up

Like I said, cleaning up after a bunch of drunk people sucks. I do it every night, but I feel like it's a million times worse when it's in your own home. Because, for as much as it wears me down to do it at work, at least I don't have to sleep there.

As a guest, don't offer to help clean up; do it. Gather some empties, put them in the recycling, and take out the trash. The host is going to remember you as the person they enjoy having in their home, because you treat their home like your own home and not like a dive bar. See how easy that is?

DRINKING AT WORK

Unless you've worked in a bar or restaurant, drinking at work is probably a foreign idea to you. That's because in this day and age, drinking in an office is a pretty weird concept. Day-drinking is seriously frowned upon, so the idea of lubing the potential clients up with a couple of martinis before the big pitch has been left back in the previous century. And rightfully so.

Drinking around the people you spend that much time with creates all sorts of problems that we could all do without. The combination of stressful hours, close proximity, and familiarity is like a bucket of gasoline, and alcohol is an open flame.

But there's also no stopping it. We're going to want to have a drink together to unwind, because otherwise work is nothing more than a place we're at for eight to ten hours a day between drinks. But great care should be taken when doing so.

Drinking with Coworkers

It's a time-honored tradition: getting together with the people you work with, consuming copious quantities of alcohol, and complaining about work. Drew Carey said it best: "Oh, you hate your job? . . . There's a support group for that. It's called EVERYBODY. They meet at the bar." It's normal and healthy, and I think it's an important part of working.

But too much of a good thing, as we all know, comes with consequences. So you've got to approach this with some caution.

The most important rule about drinking with colleagues is that you should always remember to stay in your caste if you're going to be doing any serious drinking. You don't get drunk around the people above you or the people below you. For example: If you're a professor, you don't get drunk around your students and you don't get drunk around the president of the university. If you're an attorney, you don't get drunk around the firm's partners and you don't get drunk with the paralegals. It's that simple.

Drinking with the Boss

If you're having a drink with the boss outside of work, the boss is the pace car. You don't pass the pace car. Let the boss dictate how much you'll be drinking and always try to stay a drink behind, while maintaining your composure. It's okay to stop, but it's never okay to run out of gas while trying to keep up. The boss is probably the boss for a reason, and his or her drinking prowess might be one of those reasons. Proceed with caution.

And if you are the boss, this is no time to hit it hard in some feeble attempt to show off your drinking proficiency to the junior staff. Set an example for the rest of the team, know when to call it quits, and either go home or find a drink with your peers. You'll be glad you did.

Drinking at the Office

From time to time, there might be drinks poured at the office. Working in architecture firms, we would often have "Beer Thirty" on Fridays, or a special bottle would appear after landing a client or finishing a particularly large job. The temptation to have a few and unwind in this place you think of as your home away from home is real, yet should be avoided. You will end up in bed with a coworker, embarrass yourself in front of your colleagues, or damage your standing with your boss. Stop drinking after one, say your good-byes, and unwind with a drink in your real home.

Drinking with Clients

Sometimes you're in charge of showing a client or potential client a good time. This isn't an opportunity for you to demonstrate your ability to drink. Let them determine the course of the night, and keep up as best you can. But remember that even while entertaining clients, you're on the clock. So be mindful of that when drinking.

There are drinks you can order from a bartender that don't call attention to the fact that you're ordering a low-proof cocktail. An Americano (Campari, sweet vermouth, and soda water) is a good one, as is just about any lower-proof aperitif on the rocks with a splash of soda. "Lillet on the rocks, with a splash of soda" doesn't scream out "low proof" to everyone in your party, but it does the job without a big alcoholic punch.

You should always part ways before you really want to. The point is for them to think you're headed home to do some more work before going to bed. Always be the first to leave when entertaining clients. And when you do, go straight home and treat yourself to a nightcap there if you must. You don't want to run into the people you just said good-bye to an hour earlier when you're deep in your cuffs at the tavern on the way home.

DRINKING AND SPORTS

To those who are sports fans, the sports bar is a sacred space. You treat the bar as such or you run the risk of facing a room full of agitated sports fans. And take it from me, there's nothing worse than a room full of angry sports fans.

You should be able to tell immediately if you've just walked into a bar full of fans, and if they're in the middle of watching an important game, you'll definitely know by the matching outfits and the fact that they're all screaming in unison at the television. So don't ask that one of the TVs be changed over to whatever it is that you were hoping to watch. You're outnumbered and you picked the wrong bar. Go find someplace else or watch the game at home.

Really Drink a Bloody Mary

I'm ashamed to admit it, but I have never been to the great state of Wisconsin. And the reason I'm ashamed to admit this is because for the past two decades, I have been absolutely enamored with Wisconsin drinking culture. I've talked extensively about my love of the brandy old-fashioned, the ubiquitous supper club, and the blended Grasshopper milkshake. And, still, I've never been.

The reason for my massive crush on the way Wisconsin drinks comes from my first bartending job. It was a little corner neighborhood tavern, you know the type. Neon beer signs, wood paneling, cheap cold beer on draft, a fireplace, and a couple of television sets.

You know the saying about catching more flies with honey? Well, you can catch a bunch of Wisconsinites with a neighborhood tavern. Our best and favorite regulars were a large group of folks from Wisconsin who had all either moved out West together or met when they arrived. Regardless, they were drawn to the bar, and I was drawn to them. As is common with bartenders and good regulars, we eventually became friends, and soon I was spending my weekends with these fine folks as they were teaching me how to drink properly.

Now, I don't mean that they were teaching me how to drink a lot, but rather, I was learning how to drink well. Because nobody—and I mean nobody—drinks as well as people from Wisconsin. And Wisconsinites are at their very best, better at drinking than everyone else in the world, when the Green Bay Packers are playing.

Drinking during a football game is a lot trickier than most people think it is. To the uninitiated, it seems simple: game's on, you drink beer. Right? Wrong. See, ostensibly you had some drinks the night before, and you're feeling every one of them the morning of the game. So the idea of opening up a beer for anything other than dumping into a pot with some brats and onions is pretty much repulsive. So you begin with a Bloody Mary.

I learned from my Wisconsin friends that the proper way to serve a Bloody Mary is with a small sidecar of beer. A beer back, if you will. Now, this beer doesn't tend to be very fancy—something more along the lines of pale yellow fizzy American beer. But if you're the type who enjoys a porter or pale ale with your Bloody Mary, don't let me stop you. At my bars, we always serve our Bloody Mary or Caesar with a small glass of the local lager we have on draft. But if you're out and about, you can just order yours with a beer back. You'll get what you need.

You can sip the beer as a chaser if you want, but the professional's move is to add a little bit of beer to the drink. With every sip, I replace what I took out with a little bit of beer. Beer does a great job of cutting through the thickness of a Bloody Mary; its slightly sour, bitter flavor tempers the sweet tomato juice as it mingles with the spices and adds a touch of carbonation to what is, by design, a heavy, flat cocktail.

Anyway, soon you're drinking a Bloody Mary with a heavy dose of beer in it. Once you're at the bottom of the glass, you've got some really flavorful ice, the perfect base to lay a can of tomato juice and a small beer on top of. Now what you're drinking is essentially a Red Eye, or a Spicy Red Beer. No matter what you call it, it's a step down in proof from the (hopefully) vodka-heavy Bloody Mary.

By now you've probably got a healthy buzz (you should be eating while partaking in this ritual) and you're certainly reacclimated to the taste of beer, so it's time to take off the training wheels and start drinking beer. The game's about to start.

Drinking at the Ballpark

Drinking at the ballpark is really expensive. That's why we tailgate. The drinks are better, they're cheaper, and you can hang out before the game. And hey, we've all smuggled booze into the game. I think it's actually kind of a tradition. But show a modicum of control and limit it to an airplane bottle, you cretin. Drinking from a hollowed-out cell phone, a fake sunscreen bottle, or a phony colostomy bag is just lame. It's also going to get you thrown out when you're that one guy in every section who's way too hammered to be in public. And smuggling a liter of vodka inside of a Fiji water bottle is a recipe for disaster, so don't even try it.

There are essentially two types of tailgating: warm weather tailgating (this also goes for summer concerts) and cold weather tailgating. And I'm going to give you the magic solution that works for both.

The tailgate bar kit is centered around a single pre-mixed syrup that can be tailored to each type of season.

Once you have your Tailgate Syrup (page 147) made, it's easy to whip up drinks in the parking lot.

tailgate syrup

1 cup honey

1 cup boiling water

½ cup fresh ginger, chopped

3 Tbsp allspice dram or pimento dram (available at specialty liquor stores)

1 cup freshly squeezed lemon juice, finely strained

makes enough for 24 servings

This spicy ginger syrup works in both hot and cold beverages and is incredibly easy to make.

Combine the honey, water, ginger, and allspice dram in a blender and blend on high for 1 minute. Strain the mixture through a fine strainer into a glass measuring cup and let cool. Add the lemon juice to the mixture and stir. Using a funnel, transfer to a bottle, seal, and refrigerate for up to 1 week.

FOR COLD-WEATHER TAILGATING: I bring along a cigarette-plug hot-water kettle. Equal 1½ oz portions of syrup and spirit (bourbon, scotch, dark rum, and apple brandy all work well) and 4 oz of boiling water in a heatproof mug make a perfect hot toddy.

FOR WARM-WEATHER TAILGATING: All you need is some chilled club soda and the booze of your choosing. In your favorite tailgate cup, pour 1½ oz of the syrup, 1½ oz of spirit (vodka works well, as does bourbon), and 4 oz of chilled club soda over ice for a spicy mule.

Drinking on the Golf Course

I'm not a very good golfer. Let's just get that out of the way. For every nine holes I play (and I can usually only play nine before I want to quit and head back to the clubhouse), I can only hope to have one good drive, one good chip, and one good putt. And the other sixty strokes are pretty much garbage. Yeah, you read that right. I'm bad.

But man, there is not much better than walking around a beautiful golf course on a crystal-clear afternoon, playing a little golf, and drinking an ice-cold beer. Golf is like the very best of sports and drinking combined. And when it's all over, there's a big glass of whiskey waiting for you.

Some courses have a drink cart that comes around, usually piloted by a perky young lady who is doomed to spend her summer driving around serving overpriced beer to creepy golf guys. But they're never around when you need one, and it's stupidly expensive. I usually just bring my own.

If you're gonna rent a golf cart, just fill a small cooler with cans of beer and top it off with ice. There's even a little basket on the back of every golf cart to hold it all.

If you're walking, things get a little more tricky. You obviously don't want to carry around a heavy cooler full of ice and beer, but you probably still want at least three cold beers in your bag. I mean, there's even a handy long pocket that will hold as many cans of beer as you can probably drink.

There are flexible coolers that can hold a few beers and some ice, but they're usually the wrong shape to fit in the shoe compartment of your bag. So here's what I do: Most grocery stores and department stores have a rack of long plastic bags by the front door so you can stash your wet umbrella. Next time you see one of those racks, grab a couple of the umbrella sleeves.

I just slide a few beers in one of those, fill it with ice, tie it closed, and I'm on my way. And when I get to the course, Thermos makes this thing called a Stainless Steel Beverage Can Insulator that's designed to keep a 12 oz can cold for, like, three hours. And it's ten bucks. Of course, if it takes you three hours to drink a can of beer, we need to talk.

Save the whiskey for the end of the game. Trust me on this one. You can have a nice glass at the bar at the clubhouse, which is almost always named "The Nineteenth Hole" (that's a rule). Or you can pack a little flask in your bag and have a nip on the last green. That's one of my favorite moves—a little sip of something nice shared among the group before putting out. Drinking is a ceremony, golf is all about ceremony, so it's a match made in heaven.

DRINKING ON THE ROAD

And no, not like that. Under no circumstances do you ever drink and drive, nor do you drink while driving. Road soda? Seriously? That shit is not cool. I'm old enough to remember a time when our nation's dads, captaining station wagons full of my generation's youth, would brazenly pluck cans of beer from coolers on bench seats and center consoles, drink them while cruising at top speed, and toss them out the window into our national parks. Yeah, it's kinda funny to laugh about now, given the fact that we're all alive to laugh about it. I mean, we didn't even have seat belts back then. But I'm careening off topic here.

Having a drink on the road these days is kept to the time we spend in airports and hotels, on trains, and sometimes even in tents. Let's face it, travel sucks, and everyone knows it. The way that you can tell that traveling sucks is because alcohol is provided at every step of the way. It's not there because traveling is a party. It's there because the entire experience is awful and you want to forget it.

I travel a lot for my job. Whether I'm doing a staff training in Berlin or touring in support of this book in Kansas City, I've spent enough time getting to know the right (and wrong) ways to have a drink on the road. So here's what I've learned.

Drinking at the Airport

There's a reason why every third business at the airport (right between the chair massage place and the "newsstand" that stocks more varieties of Sun Chips than actual newspapers) is a bar. Because between the line at the curb, the line at security, and the line to get on a cramped, stuffy aluminum tube, airports suck. And alcohol helps makes things suck a little less.

There's a fine line between drinking to relax and being too drunk to navigate the way to your seat. Timing is everything, so if you make it through security more quickly than you planned, take a lap around the airport before you belly up to the bar for a relaxation session.

But since getting somewhere earlier than planned is a pretty far-fetched scenario, it's much more likely that time is of the essence. Airport bars are notoriously stingy with the pours, so this is one of the only acceptable times to order a double. Typically, ordering a double is in poor taste and usually a red flag for any attentive barkeep, but at the airport it's actually encouraged. You might even be offered a schooner of beer with a questionable microbrew pedigree for an extra two bucks.

It's expensive to drink at the airport, and you don't want to risk going through security smelling like a hobo. So if you need to pack a few mini bottles in your TSA-approved toiletry bag or resealable plastic bag and drink them in a bathroom stall before your flight, you may do so in shame. Just kidding. Don't do that.

Drinking on an Airplane

Sometimes I get on an airplane and feel like I'm James Bond in an economy-class seat. But despite the temptation to tie on a pretty healthy buzz, I've got to remind myself of a few things. First off, all that recycled air is pretty dehydrating. And speaking of dehydrating, having to go through the ordeal of getting up to pee on a regular basis (see "Hangover," page 16) isn't doing you any favors either.

Not to mention that your drink options while stuck on a plane are pretty grim. You're pretty much limited to the dive-bar drink-order rules (see page 99), or you can risk being thrown off the plane, fined, arrested, or all of the above by bringing your own drinks on board. Or you can bring along a kit and use it to dress up the cards you've been dealt.

Here's what lives in my airplane cocktail kit: nothing more than a few honey sticks (you know, those clear plastic straws full of honey) and a 30 ml dropper bottle I picked up on Amazon and filled with my favorite bitters. There's nothing perishable here, and I can keep it all in my toiletry bag for the next trip. To assemble a delicious cocktail, I simply order a scotch on the rocks with a lemon and a cup of water. Here's what you do.

Drink the cup of water. You're going to want it for hydration anyway but you also need the spare cup. In that empty water cup, add three dashes of bitters and the contents of one of the honey sticks. Pour in the scotch and give the whole mess

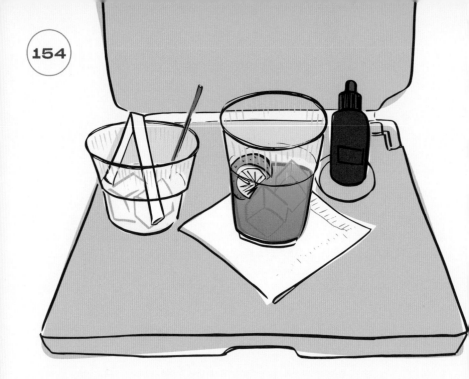

a stir with the straw or stir stick they handed you. Squeeze that lemon over the top and drop it in there, add as much or as little ice as you want, and now you've got a pretty perfect scotch old-fashioned to sip.

Voilà, a fancy cocktail at 30,000 feet. And you didn't have to break the law in order to do it.

DRINKING TO VACATION

I know I say this a lot, but vacation time is really meant for drinking (no, *you* have a problem). Margaritas on the beach? That's almost never a bad idea, unless you're pulling them out of the swim-up bar at fifteen bucks a pop. And even then, it's like, who hasn't done that at least once?

Lately, though, I've been skipping the all-inclusive resort package and just making drinks myself. It's easy and cheaper than drinking no-name liquor off a gun and I end up with a better drink than I would get at the hotel bar. And, I enjoy the reward that comes from having a drink made at my own hand. It's about all the work I want to do when I'm on vacation.

Drinking in a Hotel Room or Vacation Rental

Packing a cocktail kit full of mini-bottles of various vermouths, spirits, liqueurs, syrups, and bitters, as well as shakers and spoons in your checked luggage is an awesome option for the discerning cocktail enthusiast. And it can be done in a pretty compact package. Following is my standard travel bar kit.

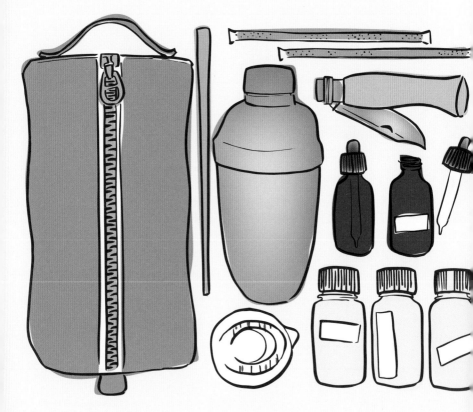

ONE 500 ML STAINLESS-STEEL COBBLER SHAKER: A cobbler contains a built-in strainer, so the need for separate tools is eliminated.

ONE COMPACT FOLDING KNIFE: I like an Opinel picnic knife (remember, this is going in your checked baggage).

ONE OR TWO TYPES OF BITTERS: Use 1 oz/30 ml dropper bottles for old-fashioneds and Sazeracs.

ONE PLASTIC CHOPSTICK: Use in lieu of a proper (and heavier) bar spoon.

HONEY STICKS: Use the kind that are a clear straw full of honey and sealed at both ends.

ONE OXO GOOD GRIPS CLEAR-PLASTIC JIGGER: Lightweight, easy to use, and has both Imperial and metric measurements.

RICH SIMPLE SYRUP (PAGE 127) AND VARIOUS LIQUEURS AND SPIRITS: Decant into mini-bottles or refillable Nalgene containers (they sell an eight-piece "travel kit" meant for toiletries that's perfect for the traveling bartender).

AN INEXPENSIVE TRAVEL DOPP KIT: Ideal for packing everything in.

With this basic setup I can make pretty much any drink I want while relaxing in my room. If there's no market nearby, I can usually procure citrus from a hotel bar with a wink, handshake, and a few bucks and juice it with my fingers. And ice at any hotel or vacation rental is usually plentiful, as is glassware.

And when I'm traveling with someone, a well-made cocktail sipped in the hotel room while we're getting ready for dinner is a pretty nice way to start an evening.

Drinking and Camping

Years ago, we had this annual boy's weekend where a bunch of bartenders would get together, drive out to middle-of-nowhere Oregon, and spend three days drinking, fishing, drinking, eating, drinking, and making fun of each other around a campfire. The women in our lives didn't understand it, but as a man, you're basically looking for any excuse to act like a moron on a daily basis. And this was the one time of year when many of us were allowing ourselves to do just that.

The camping trip was a gauntlet of drinking; a time to demonstrate some meaningless prowess over the others in the group. Everything was a contest: who could drink the most beer, who could stay up the latest while drinking, who would be the one to finish the bottle of bourbon passed around the fire at the end of the night.

This was right when I was getting into making good drinks. And I thought, well, let's start this out right. I'm going to make a gallon of delicious margaritas for the trip, with fresh juice instead of sour mix, 100 percent agave tequila in place of Sauza Gold, and Cointreau in place of cheap triple sec. Really knock it out of the park and show these guys drinking, done right.

I unveiled the precious gallon on Friday afternoon as we were setting up the campsite. It seemed like a good idea at the time. Enjoy a nice margarita, set up the tents in the hot summer sun, maybe take a refreshing dip in the lake before dinner. That's what was going through my mind.

I had temporarily forgotten the rule that we were there to drink each other under the (picnic) table because I was wholly unprepared for the scene that followed. We attacked this gallon of cocktails like it was the wild boar in *The Lord of the Flies*. "Boisterous" wouldn't even begin to describe this group. Within what seemed like minutes, people were hurling insults, laughing hysterically, and completely ignoring the reality that we needed to set up tents, you know, to sleep in after nightfall.

People were jumping in the lake fully clothed, eating *all* the food we'd brought for the weekend, and our friend Tony alienated everyone in the group and passed out next to a tree stump by five PM. It was absolute carnage, and I learned a few things that day. First, and most important, my Gallon of Margaritas recipe (page 160) is lethal. They're so delicious that you don't even think about the sheer volume of alcohol you're consuming. They're deceptively strong—lying-about-it-to-your-face strong.

The other thing I learned was that being next-level hungover in the middle of a forest is really awful. Sure, there's a cool mountain lake to jump into, but that hardly mitigates the fact that you slept on the ground with a rock poking you in the spine all night. It's brutal, and there's no convenience store across the street with Gatorade and Advil. It's just you and your suffering.

gallon of margaritas

6 cups good reposado tequila (that's a little under two-fifths)

2½ cups Cointreau (about 5 oz shy of a full fifth)

2½ cups freshly squeezed lime juice

2½ cups freshly squeezed lemon juice

1½ cups Rich Simple Syrup (see page 127)

1 cup water

makes about
20 servings

If you can't find a one-gallon beverage dispensing cooler, you can just buy a gallon of distilled water from the grocery store for under a buck and use the water for your plants.

Mix the tequila, Cointreau, lime juice, lemon juice, simple syrup, and water together in a gallon container. Don't forget to refrigerate! The mixture should stay fresh for up to 4 days. When ready to serve, pour over ice into old-fashioned glasses, camping cups, or red Solo cups.

So, whatever you do, make sure you warn the group before you serve these margaritas. And if you're taking them camping, know what you're in for and drink accordingly.

Drinking Around Water

I grew up in California, which means I spent a lot of time in the water. That's just how it goes there. We lived about ten minutes from the beach, but I grew up on swim team. We were a third-generation swim team family—Mom was a swimmer, and Grandma was a swimmer, too. I hope my nephew keeps the streak going and becomes a swimmer one day.

If you're thinking that this is going to be a story wherein you learn how to sneak alcohol into a public pool via a sunscreen container, you couldn't be more wrong. You have so many options for poolside drinking—you can go to Vegas, you can go to a friend's house, or you can even get a cheap hotel for the night. But there's something really unwholesome and just kind of gross about drunk adults in a child's domain, like a playground or public pool. There are places where you don't need to have a drink, and I think it's fair to look down on people who think they do.

Outside of that, there is one cardinal rule that must be obeyed whenever you consume alcohol (or any type of beverage, really) around water, and that's NO GLASS. I don't know why people don't take this rule more seriously. It's that important. You have people running around in very little clothing and bare feet, and you know that anything made of glass will eventually break (see page 135). Combining those two things is a very, very bad idea. So if you're going to have some drinks, make sure that they're transported in either aluminum cans or plastic. Don't even bring a glass bottle of wine to the pool and drink it out of plastic cups. Just keep the glass containers at home. Please.

When I was just out of college, my friend Tom bought a ski boat. I wasn't really working in architecture firms yet, as I kinda took the summer off to keep working in bars and, well, party. School was tough, and I was happy to be done. We both worked nights, and I was only working, like, three or four shifts a week, so most days we would spend out on the lake, wakeboarding and drinking, listening to classic rock, and having a hell of a time.

Tom took water safety very seriously, which I'm thankful for today because, well, I'm not dead. Being drunk on or around a body of water is a recipe for disaster. You think, "I'm a strong swimmer, I'm not going to drown," but there are so many other factors, the main one being that drunk people are super prone to (a) falling down and (b) hitting their heads on things. And people who hit their heads on things are almost always in for trouble when there's water nearby.

But, hey, there have got to be some drinks if you're hanging out on the lake, river, pool, or ocean, right? For sure. But that's why I always like to keep it low proof when I do so. Blended drinks are kinda perfect for just this occasion, since they tend to be inherently lower proof. The Shandy, that delicious beer and lemonade mixture, is a perfect beach sipper. I pack an equal number of six-pack cans of Sanpellegrino Limonata and my favored light lager du jour and mix them in large plastic cups. Feeling more like a grapefruit Radler? Sanpellegrino makes a grapefruit soda as well that pairs perfectly with beer.

But, sure, sometimes you have to smuggle alcohol into a situation where you're not normally permitted to do so. And, no, I'm not talking about the public pool. I'm talking about cruise ships. Major cruise lines survive on cheap ticket prices and selling you really expensive booze when you get in there. So a lot of the big companies search your luggage for alcohol because they don't want you smuggling it in. You can, you just need to do some research.

If the cruise ship you're planning on boarding allows water bottles with unbroken seals, all you need to do is search Amazon.com for 28 mm tamper-resistant screw caps. Then you can fill all of the plastic bottles you want with the clear liquid of your choice, seal with a new, unbroken tamper-resistant cap, and you're ready to go. Don't say I never did anything for you.

Drinking Abroad

I could fill an entire book of local drinking customs of every region in the world. But I'm not going to be able to do that here. So this is what you need to remember when you're traveling: It's always a good idea to make every attempt to learn the local customs. Is it rude to signal the waiter in the country you'll be visiting? Is it weird to fill your own glass before your guest's?

Questions like these are easy to look up on the internet, so if you're traveling and you know you'll be taking in some of the local flavors, just do your due diligence and make an attempt to fall in line with the local social cues. This world would be a better place if we all tried to be more respectful of each other, and we may as well start when we're drinking. Because the act of having a drink is one of the oldest and most human rituals on the planet, and doing it well, and with respect to everyone around you, is the sign of a truly civilized individual. Cheers to you.